CLASSIC
BEADED PURSE
PATTERNS

E. de Jong-Kramer

Kangaroo Press

Photography: Hans van Ommeren, Woerden
Diagrams: E. de Jong-Kramer, Midlum
   Hetty Paërl, Amsterdam
Design: Karel van Laar, de Bilt
English translation: Tina Llowarch

Cover: Purse from Wouterswoude (see page 51)

Frontispiece: The bird (see page 47)

© Cantecleer bv, de Bilt 1986

© English translation Kangaroo Press 1996

This edition first published in 1996 by Kangaroo Press
an imprint of Simon & Schuster (Australia) Pty Limited
20 Barcoo Street, East Roseville NSW 2069

A Viacom Company
Sydney New York London Toronto Tokyo Singapore

Printed in Hong Kong by South China Printing Co. (1988) Ltd

ISBN 0 86417 769 0

10 9 8 7 6 5 4

Contents

1 Introduction 6

2 Techniques 8

Technique A 8
Looped purse 8

Technique B 11
Apache purse 11
Spider or spider's web 14
Spider with crochet 15
Diamond purse 16

Technique C 16
Doll purse 16
Star purse with five-pointed star 19

Purl knitting 23
Finishing off 23
Shaping 24
Lining and attaching the handles 24

3. Patterns 25

Black and white purse: Wouterswoude
(Forest of the hunters) 27
Black and white purse: Bird on a
branch 29
Leeuwarden (Lion's heart) 30
Eewal (Weir on the lake) 32
Oostermeer (Eastern lake) 34
Rose with orange flower 35
Black and white purse: Flower with
border 37
Faith, hope and charity 39
Wieringen (from Lake Wier) 41
Crayfish 43

Blue flower 45
Purple dahlia 46
The bird 47
Glasses holder 48
Nel 50
Wouterswoude (Forest of the
hunters) 51
Dog with fluffy tail 53
Deer 55

Explanation of symbols 56
Acknowledgments 56

1. Introduction

Beads have recently become fashionable again. They are available in innumerable variations, sizes, colours and composition. Beads can be used in a multitude of different ways as decoration: by threading them into jewellery, by sewing onto fabrics and garments and by incorporating them into different articles using techniques such as tatting, macrame, crochet and knitting. Over tens of thousands of years, beads have been used by many cultures in many ways. They form a fascinating area of study.

Antique beaded purses can still be found in many different parts of the Netherlands. Discussions with local collectors can lead to the discovery of many fine examples, with both clasps and drawstrings, that have been collected over the years.

Purse patterns and clasp designs belonged to particular population groups and formed part of the economic culture. The old saying about having 'a thin or a fat purse' is still used; and it used to be said that the wider and more expensive the clasp on the purse was, the richer the owner of that purse would be.

Through the medium of pattern and colour the way of life of each particular region was expressed, many designs and colours being connected to specific areas. The province of North Holland, for example, was noted for its rose patterns; along the coast the purses displayed fishing boats and the area of Kamper Island was famous for its different shades of blue. Beads were available in many shades of the colour blue, perhaps because blue was thought to have a protective quality.

If you were to delve into the background of beaded purses, bags, clasps and handles, you would be amazed at how little knowledge has been preserved. Apparently the basic patterns were often added to with different motifs, which could have come from cross-stitch pattern books. Evidence for this is seen in purses which have the same central flower pattern, but totally different patterns in the borders at top and bottom.

Working with beads is not only a pleasant way to spend some recreational time, it can lead to many social contacts, and the work itself can have a therapeutic effect. Young and old can gain a great deal of pleasure from making beaded purses.

At the present time it is very difficult to find suitable materials and authentic patterns for making beaded purses; this book has been designed to give a helping hand to those people who may wish to practise the art, both explaining the techniques for knitting with beads and providing authentic patterns to work on.

The requirements are quite simple: besides the beads, you will need a crochet hook, and one or two pairs of double-pointed knitting needles in various thicknesses to suit the yarns used for the beads. To knit very small beads [size 11] use 1.25 mm [0000] or 1.50 mm [000] knitting needles. For threading the beads use a fine twisted wire beading needle.

When working with very small beads stiffen the end of the thread by applying some glue or nail polish and twisting the thread. It is also possible to use fine copper wire such as fuse wire as a needle. Double the wire and twist it around, leaving the bend to function as an eye.

The colour of the cotton is very important, particularly when using transparent beads, as the effect will be determined by the colour of the thread. A darker thread is usually best, especially with dark coloured beads. The most suitable cotton for beading is DMC Cordonnet 40 or 60. You can also use DMC Perle Cotton No.8, in which a large range of colours is available.

Make sure before starting that the beads are colourfast. Sometimes the colour is just a painted veneer that will come off with wear. You can check this by threading a few beads on a piece of thread and leaving them in boiling water for approximately five minutes; this will demonstrate whether they are colourfast or not. A beaded article will not look very good if the beads are faded. The photos and the text will help you follow the diagrams to make your own beaded purses.

2. Techniques

There are three main techniques used for knitting beads:

A: Knitting with an extra guiding thread;
B: Knitting the beads in between the stitches;
C: Knitting a beaded thread through the stitches.

The patterns are ordered from the simplest to the most challenging; therefore it is advisable that you begin at the beginning! Each pattern is drawn from an existing purse. The motifs are quite simple to trace, but it can happen occasionally that an error is found in an old pattern. This is because most knitted purses were handmade, sometimes by children. A very old jeweller told me how his grandfather used regularly to travel to Leeuwarden to buy all sorts of bags and purses. In Leeuwarden lived a jeweller who in turn travelled to Prague to pick up the knitted work. The children there did not attend school in winter, but stayed at home and helped their mothers knit the purses using beads already threaded in a factory by male workers.
Because the beads are worked on a twisted stitch in stocking [stockinette] stitch, quite often the designs become crooked. This can be corrected by stretching the article, but it appears the old piece-workers did not always have enough time to do this—perhaps because the people contracted to attach the handles and clasps (made of real silver) did their part of the work as fast as possible, to earn more money.
In the years around 1900 the jewellers sold the purses for as little as two guldens, approximately $A1 [US$0.75] each.

Technique A
(knitting with an extra guiding thread)

The looped purse on page 10 is an example of this style. The guide thread holds the beads which are measured off with each loop. If you are starting with this purse, you may need to practise the technique of knitting with fine needles first.

Looped purse, illustration 1

Requirements
white DMC perle cotton No. 8
beads in main colour
beads in a contrasting colour
white DMC Cordonnet No. 50
4 double-pointed knitting needles 1.25 mm or 1.5 mm [000 or 0000]
beading needle

Method
Using 3 of the 4 double-pointed needles and DMC perle cotton, cast on 2 x 40 stitches = 80 stitches, divided evenly on the 3 needles to work in the round. Work 2 rounds moss stitch. Continue in stocking [stockinette] stitch, i.e. knit 1 round, purl 1 round. Work 8 rounds, increasing 4 sts in each knit round (16 sts inc), making a total of 96 stitches. Continue in stocking [stockinette] stitch for 2 more rounds.
Thread the beads needed for the round onto the DMC Cordonnet to make the loops. Each loop is made from 28 beads, divided into two colours: 13 + 2 + 13. Continue threading groups of 28 beads for

> **Colour plate 1** *Nel (above; see page 50) and a spider purse with an exquisite silver clasp, obviously the property of a well-to-do farming family*

8

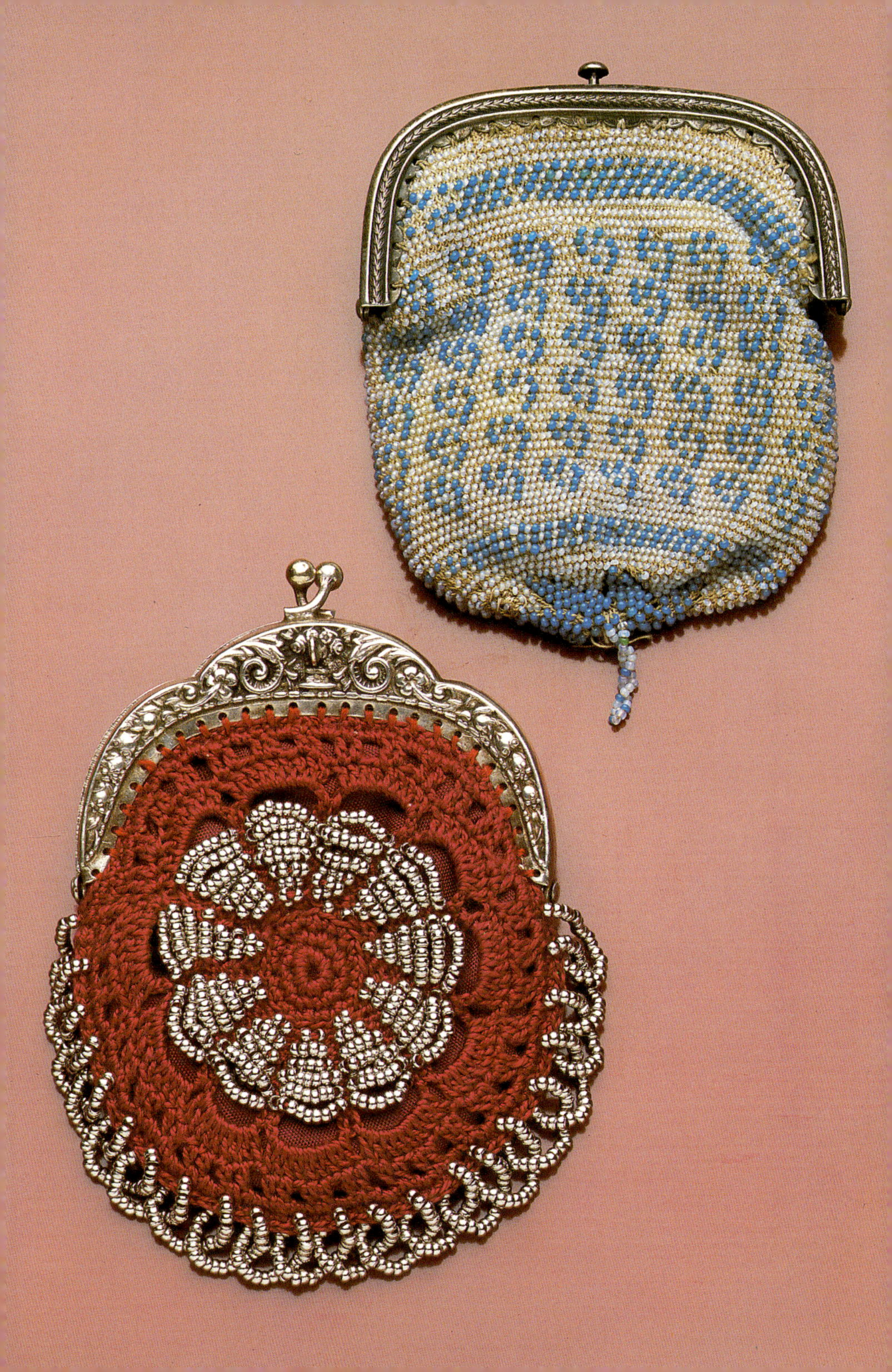

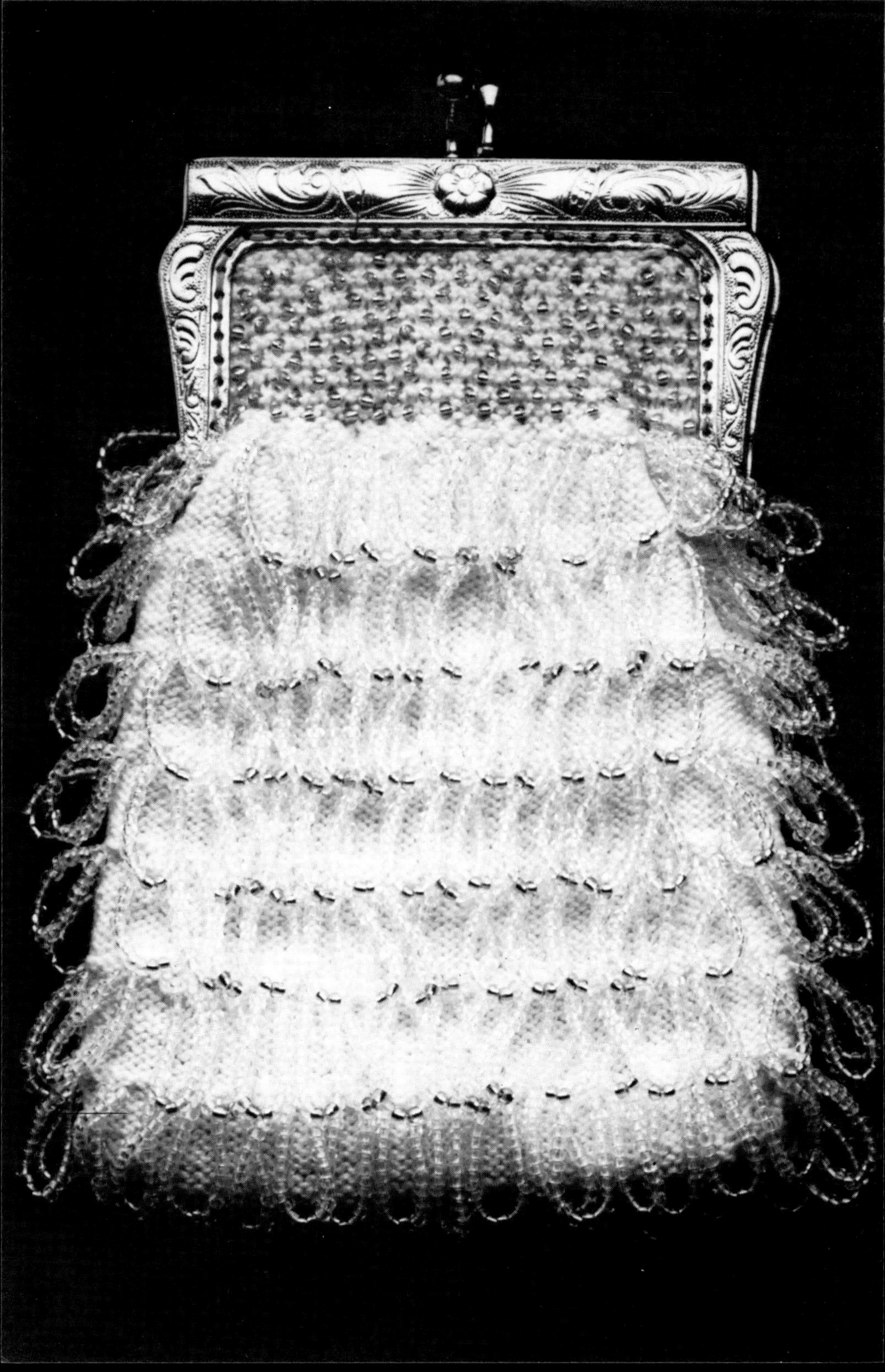

each of the 49 loops required. It is easier to count like this: 13 + 2 + (13 + 13 =) 26 + 2 + 26 + 2, etc., ending with 13 beads.
The next round is knitted with a double thread, i.e. the perle cotton No.6 and the guiding thread of DMC Cordonnet. Work as follows (beads at back of work): knit 2, * make loop of 28 beads, knit 2, rep from * to last loop of beads. The loops form on the knit side of the work.
Work 9 rounds stocking [stockinette] stitch in perle cotton No.6, then 1 round of loops. Repeat the 10 rounds until 7 looped rounds have been made, ending with a purl round.
Next round: Knit 2 together, knit 1, repeat to end (64 sts).
Turn the work inside out, loops to the outside.
To work the top part, divide the work in two. Thread beads onto perle cotton No. 6, using a little glue to stiffen the end of the cotton. Work each piece separately to the required length, depending on the size of the clasp to be used.
Using the 32 stitches work as follows: knit 1, thread 1 bead (colour 1), knit 1 twisted (tbl), 1 bead (colour 2), etc. The stitch that follows the bead is always a knit stitch twisted to enable the bead to sit straight, i.e. knitted through the back of the loop (tbl). Knit all the even rows in purl without beads. In the next row the beads are moved slightly, so that they are between the stitches. Repeat this 7 times (or the required number of times for the clasp you are using), cast off loosely.
Work the other side to match.

You can follow the pattern strictly, but it is also possible to make the pattern smaller, using half the number of stitches (i.e. 2 x 20, inc to 48), and working with 6 rows of stocking [stockinette] stitch instead of 10. The loops are made with 18 beads. Another variation on this could be to use 5 instead of 7 looped rows. In place of white cotton, coloured cotton could be used.

Technique B
(knitting with beads between the stitches)

Examples of this method are the Apache purses shown on page 13, which can be made in different sizes. If you intend to use a larger number of stitches, you will need to increase the length of the purse to preserve the shape.
With the looped purse this technique was used in the upper part: knit 1, slip on 1 bead, knit 1 tbl (to straighten the bead).

Apache purse, illustration 2

Requirements
DMC perle cotton No. 8
2 double-pointed knitting needles 1.25 mm or 1.5 mm [000 or 0000]
crochet hook 1.25 mm
beads to match cotton
beading needle

Method
Thread the required number of beads onto the perle cotton (in this instance, 2520 beads are required for the whole purse). Cast on 18 stitches. Adjust the number of stitches and the number of beads according to the size of the purse if you want the finished purse larger or smaller. For a smaller purse you can thread all the beads;

Illustration 1 *Looped purse. Looped purses are found in many different sizes and numbers of stitches. In North Holland especially, looped purses were common.*
The following story shows how carefully a housewife from Beemster looked after her purse: The purse was kept in the locked linen press, where each shelf was covered in a carefully starched and ironed lace-edged sheet. If a payment needed to be made, the housewife would lift up her overskirt and take a bunch of keys from the diesek, a purse in the shape of an open envelope sewn to her underskirt. The linen press would be unlocked and from under the sheet, wrapped in a cloth fastened with a safety pin, the beaded purse would be taken. This ritual was performed for every payment.

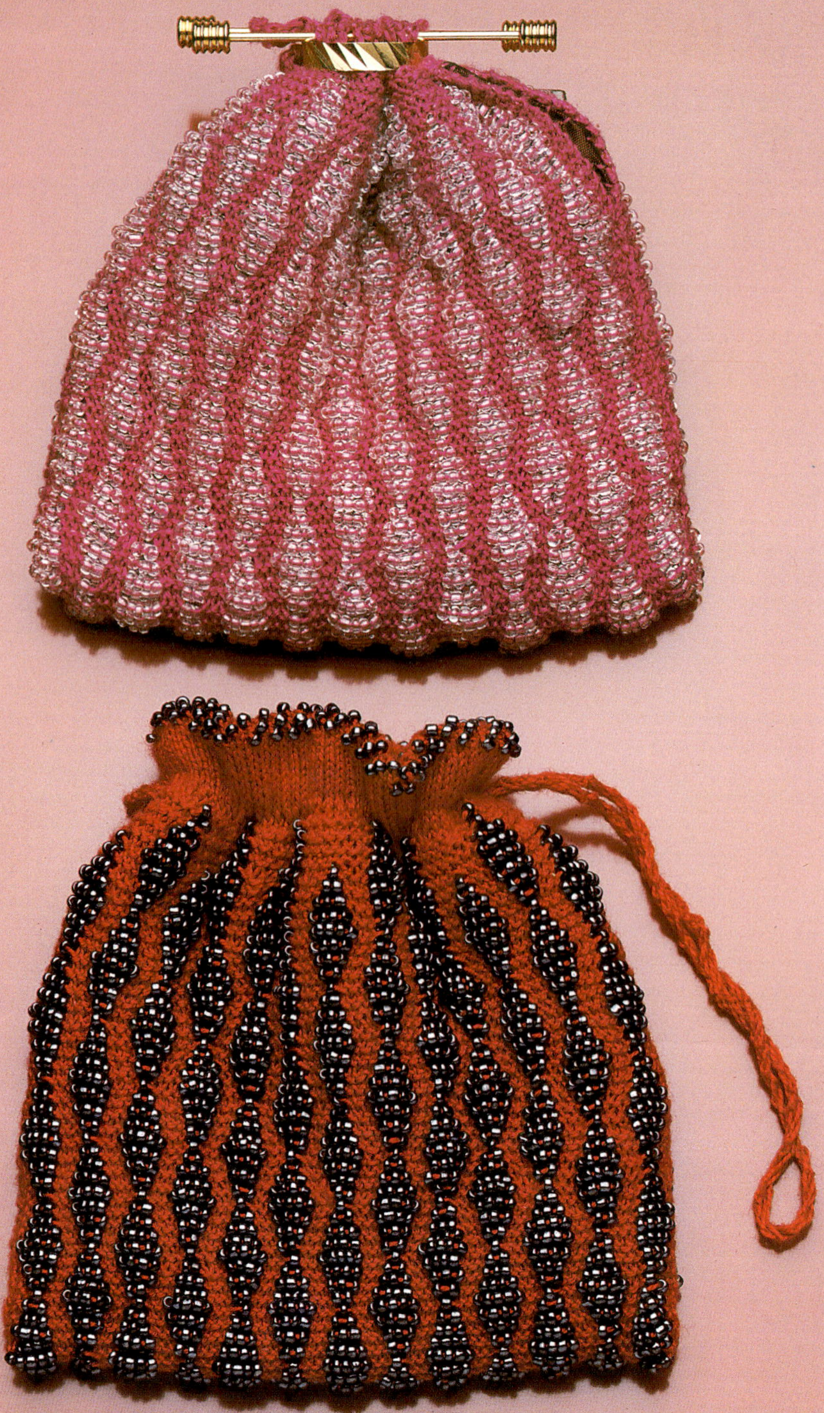

< **Colour plate 2** *Diamond purses. These purses are easily knitted with two needles. They are finished with either a clasp or a drawstring*

Illustration 2 *Apache purse. An easy-to-make purse which requires only two knitting needles*

Illustration 3 *Spider. These purses were found all over the country. The knitted work was often alternated with crochet*

for a larger purse it is easier to thread the beads in sections.

Knit three rows garter stitch, working both edges of every row with 3 knit stitches.
Continue: K3, 1 bead, k2, 1 bead, k2, 1 bead, to the end, finishing with k3 (7 beads altogether).
Note: K2 = [k1, k1 twisted (tbl)].
Work 3 more rows with 1 bead between stitches.
Continue with 4 rows with 2 beads between stitches (14 beads per row); 4 rows with 3 beads (21 beads); 6 rows with 4 beads (28 beads); 6 rows with 5 beads (35 beads); 6 rows with 6 beads (42 beads); 6 rows with 7 beads (49 beads); 6 rows with 8 beads (56 beads). These are the widest rows.
Continue for the other side, decreasing the number of beads in the same manner: 6 rows with 7 beads between stitches, 6 rows with 6 beads, 6 rows with 5 beads, 6 rows with 4 beads, 4 rows with 3 beads, 4 rows with 2 beads, 4 rows with 1 bead, finishing with 3 unbeaded rows of garter stitch. Cast off.
Make a lining and attach it to the inside. Sew both sides closed halfway. Attach the clasp last.

The second example of technique B is the spider or spider's web.

Spider or spider's web, illustration 3

Requirements
beads
DMC perle cotton No. 8 to match the beads
4 double-pointed knitting needles 1.25 mm or 1.5 mm [000 or 0000]
crochet hook 0.75 or 1.00 mm [#10 or 12]
beading needle

Method
Thread the required amount of beads, about 6 m (6½ yds). Using the crochet hook make 5 loose ch, close with a slip st to form a circle.
Make 18 tr [18 dc] into this circle. With knitting needles continue in stocking [stockinette] stitch, working into the back of the stitch in each knit row (6 stitches on each needle).
1st row: Knit around with 1 bead between each stitch, working into the back of each stitch (tbl).
Row 2: Purl around with 1 bead between each stitch.
3rd row: Knit 1 tbl, 2 beads, knit 1 tbl, 2 beads, continue to end (remember, needle in back of stitch).
4th row: Purl 1, 2 beads, continue to end.
5th row: Knit 1 tbl, 3 beads, continue to end.
6th row: Purl 1, 3 beads, continue to end.
7th row: Knit 1 tbl, 4 beads, continue to end.
8th row: Purl 1, 4 beads, continue to end.
Continue in this way, adding beads every second row until there are 11 beads between the stitches.
Using the crochet hook pick up last knit stitch removed from needle. Make 11 or 12 loose ch [dc], connect to next knitted stitch (remove stitch from needle), make 11 or 12 loose ch, and repeat with each next knitted stitch to the end.
This makes 18 loops. Work 11 or 12 tr [dc] into each of the first 6 loops.
Make the other side of the purse in the same way.
Place the two completed sides together and join the remaining 12 loops together with treble [dc].

Make a suitable lining and attach inside the purse.
Make 13 beaded loops underneath the purse as follows: Using a beading needle, thread 23 beads and join from back to front, approximately 1 cm (5/8") along. Take the needle through the made loop and make the next loop approximately 1 cm (5/8") further along.

To make the 'Spider with crochet' the rounds are knitted singly, and crochet is used to make a border. The rounds not knitted double = 2 rnds, 2 beads; 2 rnds, 3 beads; 2 rnds, 4 beads. With the crochet pattern the bead number increases each round.

Spider with crochet, colour plate 1

Requirements
DMC perle cotton No. 8
crochet hook 0.75 or 1.00 mm [#10 or 12]
3 boxes of small beads (e.g. seed beads)
4 double-pointed knitting needles 1.25 mm or 1.5 mm [000 or 0000]

Method
First thread the beads—approximately 2 m (2¼ yds). Crochet 3 loose ch, slip st to 1st ch to form a circle. Work 3 ch, 5 dc[sc], slip st into top of 3 ch (to join) = 6 dc[sc].
2nd rnd: 3 ch, 2 dc[sc], into each dc[sc] around, slip st into top of 3 ch to join = 11 dc[sc].
3rd rnd: 3 ch, 1 dc[sc] in next st, 2 dc[sc] in next st to end, slip st to join = 22 dc[sc].
Transfer all stitches to knitting needles, picking up from the backs of the loops, making 8 - 6 - 8 stitches.
1st row: 1 bead, knit 2 (the first stitch is twisted), rep to end.
2nd row: 2 beads, knit 2, rep to end.
3rd row: 3 beads, knit 2, rep to end.
Continue in this way until there are 9 beads between the stitches.
Slip last stitch on a crochet hook and * make 9 loose ch, slip st to next knit st, rep from * all around, slip st to 1st st. Work 9 tr[dc] over each 9 ch loop, and connect these with a slip st at the end.

15

Turn work around: 3 ch, 1 tr[dc], * 2 tr[dc], 2 ch, etc. Approximately one-third of the way along the row close the stitch and cut the thread.
Work second side in the same way.
Place the two circles together and continue around bottom of bag from *, joining both sides together to end of rnd. Slip st in top of 3 ch.
To finish, sew a lining into the purse, attach bead loops as described for the spider on page 15, and sew a clasp at the top.

The third example of technique B is the diamond purse.

Diamond purse, colour plate 2

Requirements
DMC perle cotton No. 8
beads in a matching colour
2 double-pointed knitting needles 1.25 mm or 1.5 mm [000 or 0000]

Method
Thread approx. 2 m (2¼ yds) of beads.
Cast on 42 stitches.
Work 4 rows stocking [stockinette] st.
5th row: K6, 1 bead, k6, etc, finishing with k6.
6th and every alternate row: Knit.
7th row: K6, 2 beads, k6, etc.
9th row: K6, 3 beads, k6, etc.
11th row: K6, 4 beads, k6, etc.
12th row: Knit.
The number of beads in these diamonds now needs to be decreased. At the same time the next diamonds are started midway between the first diamonds. Split the groups of 6 stitches:
13th row: K6, 5 beads, k3, 1 bead, k3, 5 beads, k3, 1 bead, etc, ending with k6.
14th and every alternate row: Knit.
15th row: K6, 4 beads, k3, 2 beads, k3, 4 beads, k3, 2 beads, etc, ending with k6.
17th row: K6, 3 beads, k3, 3 beads, k3, 3 beads, k3, 3 beads, etc, ending with k6.
19th row: K6, 2 beads, k3, 4 beads, k3, 2 beads, k3, 4 beads, etc, ending with k6.
21st row: K6, 1 bead, k3, 5 beads, k3, 1 bead, k3, 5 beads, etc, ending with k6.

23rd row: K6, 2 beads, k3, 4 beads, k3, 2 beads, k3, 4 beads, etc, ending with k6.
25th row: K6, 3 beads, k3, 3 beads, k3, 3 beads, k3, 3 beads, etc, ending with k6.
27th row: K6, 4 beads, k3, 2 beads, k3, 4 beads, k3, 2 beads, etc, ending with k6.
29th row: K6, 5 beads, k3, 1 bead, k3, 5 beads, k3, 1 bead, etc, ending with k6.
Continue until you have knitted 10 whole diamonds, one under the other, in each of the vertical rows.
170th and every alternate row: Knit.
171st row: K6, 4 beads, k6, 4 beads, etc. ending with k6.
173rd row: K6, 3 beads, k6, 3 beads, etc, ending with k6.
175th row: K6, 2 beads, k6, 2 beads, etc, ending with k6.
177th row: K6, 1 bead, k6, 1 bead, etc, ending with k6.
Work 4 rows stocking [stockinette] stitch.
Cast off.
Join the sides and sew a lining into the purse, finishing with a clasp or a drawstring.

Technique C

(the beads are threaded on a thread and knitted through each stitch)

Most beaded purses are knitted following this technique. During the knitting when the thread is lifted the bead will move against the needle resting against the left forefinger and together with the thread is then pushed through the stitch. Make sure the bead sits to the front of the work. To hold the bead more firmly the stitch is twisted to the right, i.e knit into the back of the stitch. Much of this type of knitting was derived from France where apparently it was taught in prisons, being used to keep prisoners busy as well as subdued.
Using the doll purse as an example, these instructions can be used as a base for all the other purses that are knitted in the same way. In these directions you will also gain an understanding of how the beads are knitted for the larger purses.
When working with large numbers of beads

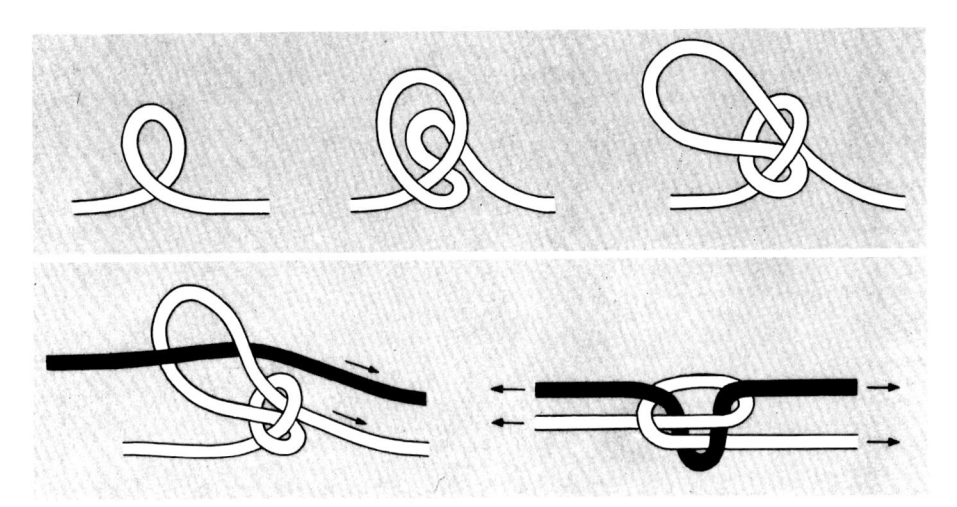

Illustration 4 *The weaver's knot*

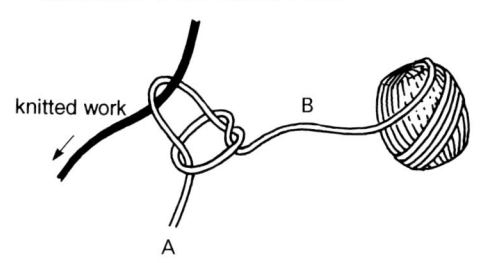

Illustration 5 *Knot*

you may end up with too many or too few beads on a thread. Too many beads are simply removed by cutting the thread carefully. If there are not enough beads, thread the required extra amount onto another length of cotton and knot the threads together with a weaver's knot (illustrations 4 and 5). Continue knitting as before.

Doll's purse, illustration 6

Requirements
DMC Cordonnet No. 50
100 g [3 oz] very small beads for the background
small amounts of coloured beads for the pattern (see chart, p. 56)
4 double-pointed knitting needles 1.00 mm or 1.25 mm [0000 or 00000]

Method 1
Because this purse is knitted in the round, the beads for the complete purse can be threaded in colour order in one operation. Starting at A (at the top of diagram 6a), thread each row twice, once for the front and once for the back. Thread twice from A to B. Thread the following row twice, from C to D. Continue threading all the following rows twice, following the diagram to E. Each symbol, including the blank squares, represents a different colour. See the chart on page 56.
Cast on 2 x 16 stitches = 32 stitches.
Work the first two rows in moss stitch, with half the stitches on one needle and the rest divided between the second and third needles (8 stitches each), with the fourth needle used for working.
Increase the number of stitches as follows: large needle—1 stitch twisted right with a bead through it, yarn over needle to increase 1 stitch, continue knitting to end of row to last stitch, yarn over needle, knit 1 (twisted right with bead through it). Continue on the two other needles in the same way.
In the following rows the yarn over needle is knitted as a stitch; 1 stitch after the start and before the end of the row make another yarn over needle, increasing in this

17

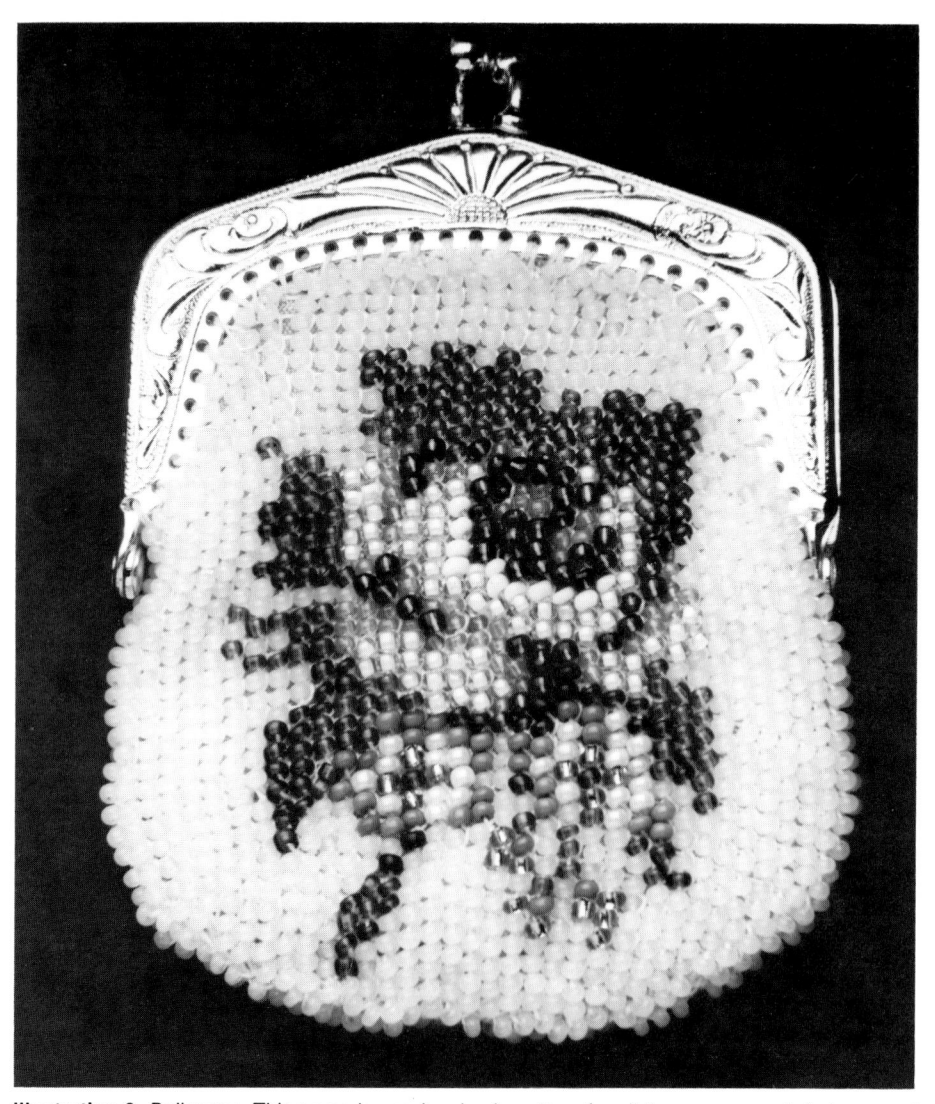

Illustration 6 *Doll purse. This purse is used as basic pattern for all the purses made in two equal pieces. Each row is threaded twice. Where the front and back pieces are not identical, the two different patterns are placed beside each other and the rows are threaded singly*

manner until there are 36 stitches on the first needle and 18 stitches on each of the others (72 stitches). Work another 20 rows without increasing.

Divide the work into two for the front and the back.

To fit the clasp decrease one stitch on both sides: k1, k2 tog, yarn over needle, k1 with bead. Continue to last 3 stitches, k2 tog, yarn over needle, k1 with bead, k1.

Continue decreasing until there are 16 stitches on each side (32 stitches). Work 2 rows of k1, p1, cast off.

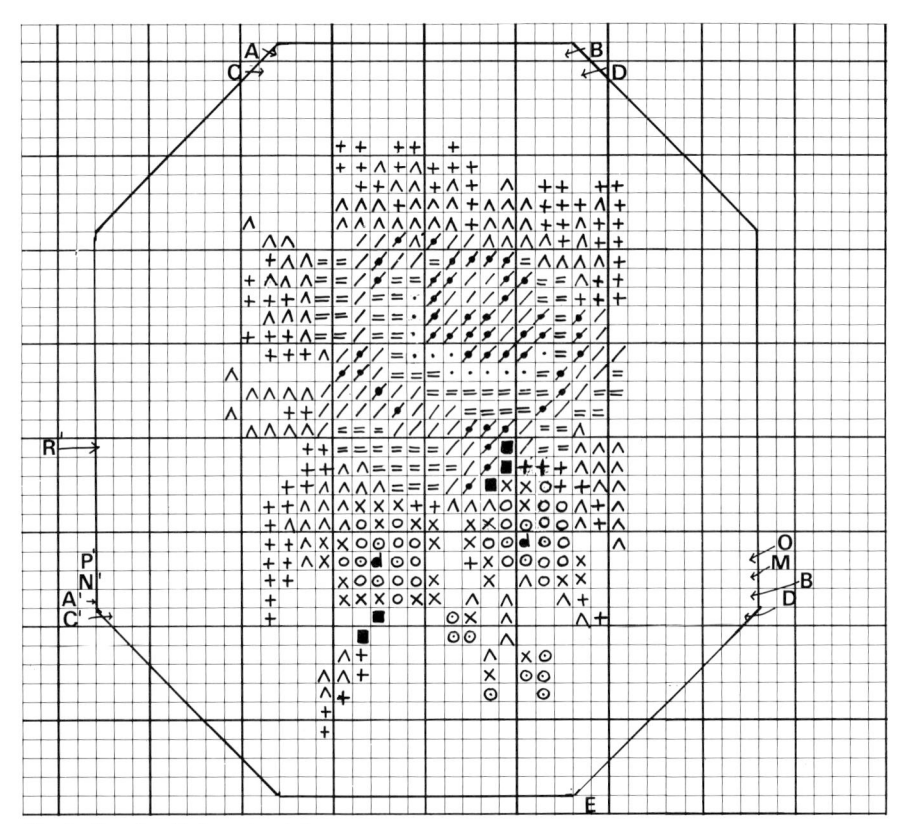

Illustration 6a *Pattern for doll purse*

Method 2
This method is usually used for making larger purses and bags. Start threading at A', thread twice from A' to B', twice from C' to D' until you reach E. Take the beading needle off the thread and work as in method 1, until you reach A'. Unwind some thread from the ball and following the diagram thread twice from the right, from M' to N' and from O' to P'. Continue threading this way until all the thread has been used. Unwind several metres (yards) from the ball and start from R, threading from left to right until you reach the point where the work was left uncompleted. Attach the thread to the knitting with a weaver's knot and finish the purse off. Decrease as in method 1.

Another example of technique C follows.

Star purse or purse with five-pointed star, illustration 7 and colour plate 3

Requirements
DMC Cordonnet No.50
beads in several different colours
4 double-pointed knitting needles 1.00 mm or 1.25 mm [0000 or 00000]

Method
This purse is knitted from the outside so you will need to decrease towards the middle. Do not decrease in the first five rows. Before starting to knit, thread the beads. Start at A at the bottom of the diagram and

19

Illustration 7a Pattern for the star purse

Illustration 7b Pattern for star purse with flower (see colour plate 3)

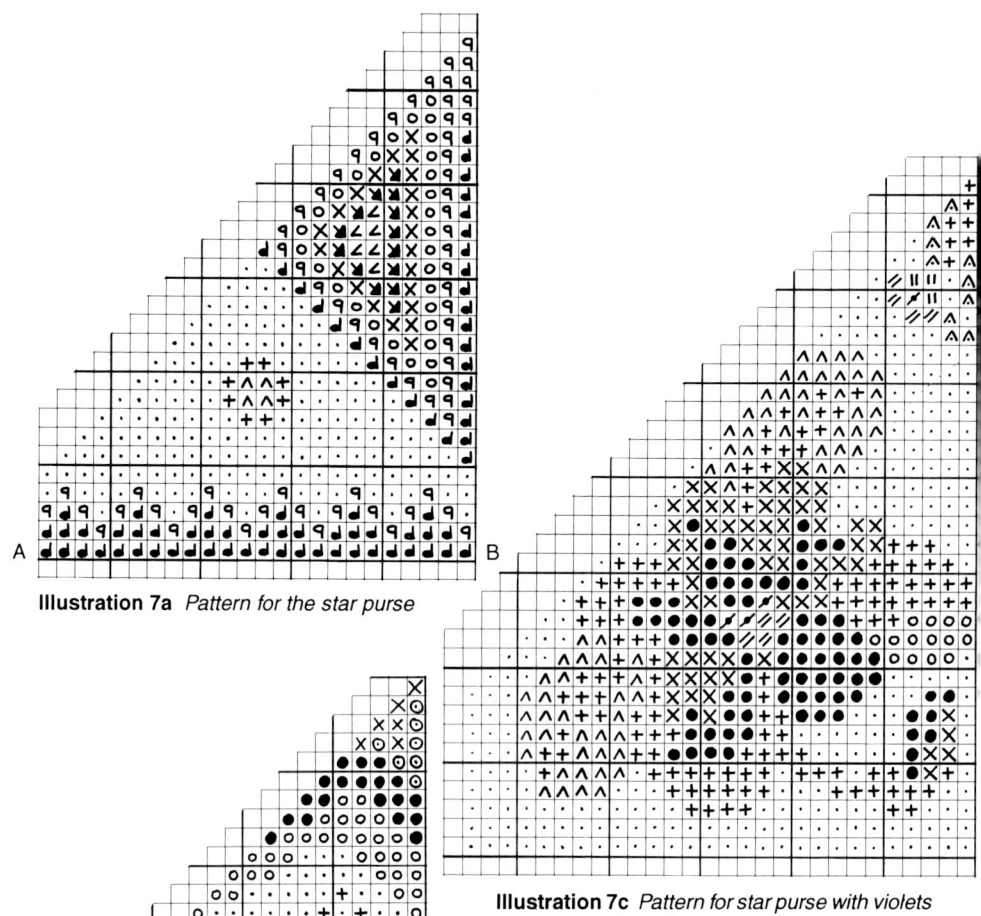

Illustration 7c Pattern for star purse with violets (see colour plate 3)

▶**Illustration 7** Star purses, found in many different areas, can be identified with a particular region by the colours used. The mathematically precise stars were made in many colour combinations, and surrounded by a variety of stylised borders. The stylised border was replaced in the nineteenth century by a more natural pattern

20

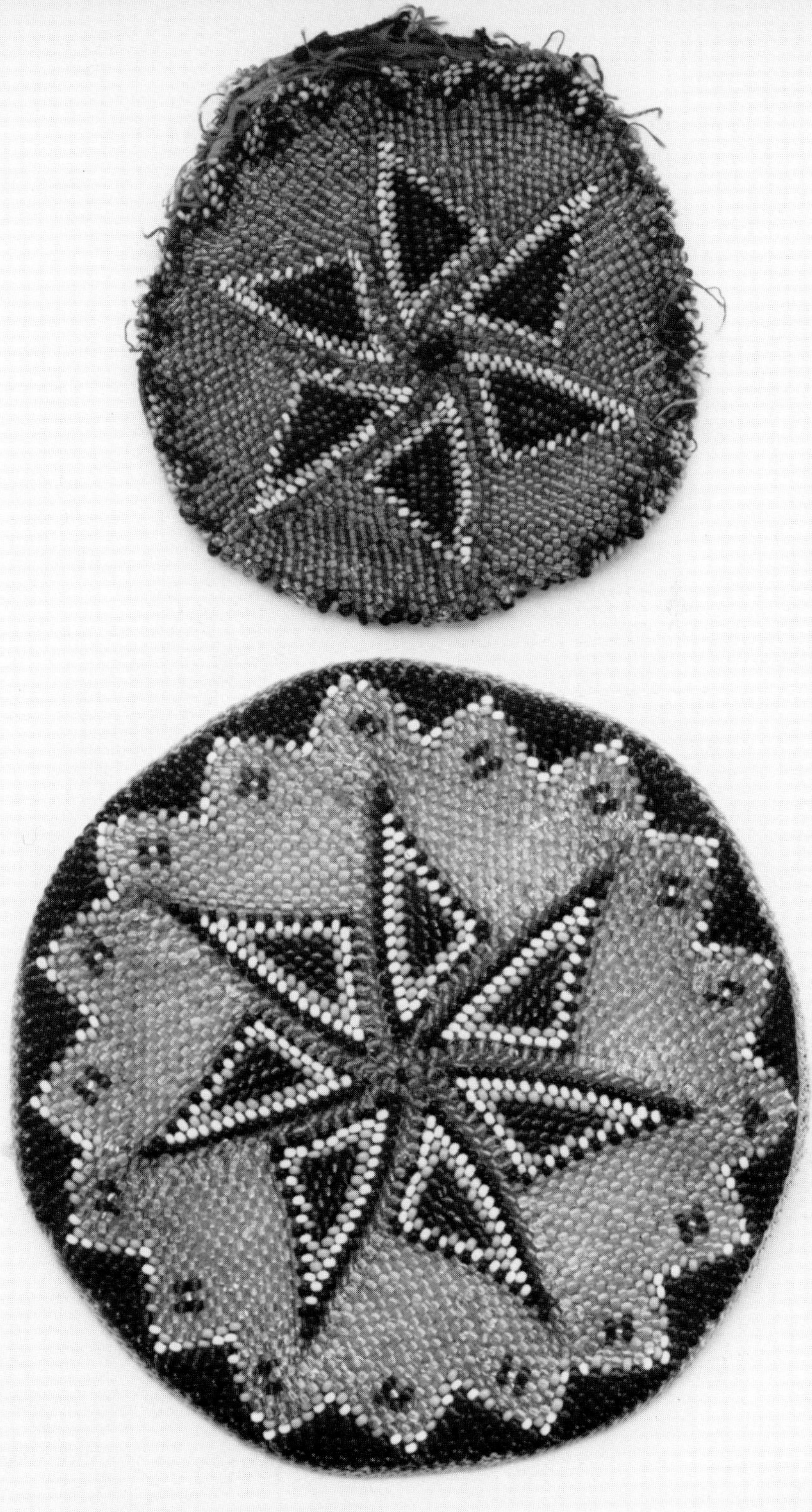

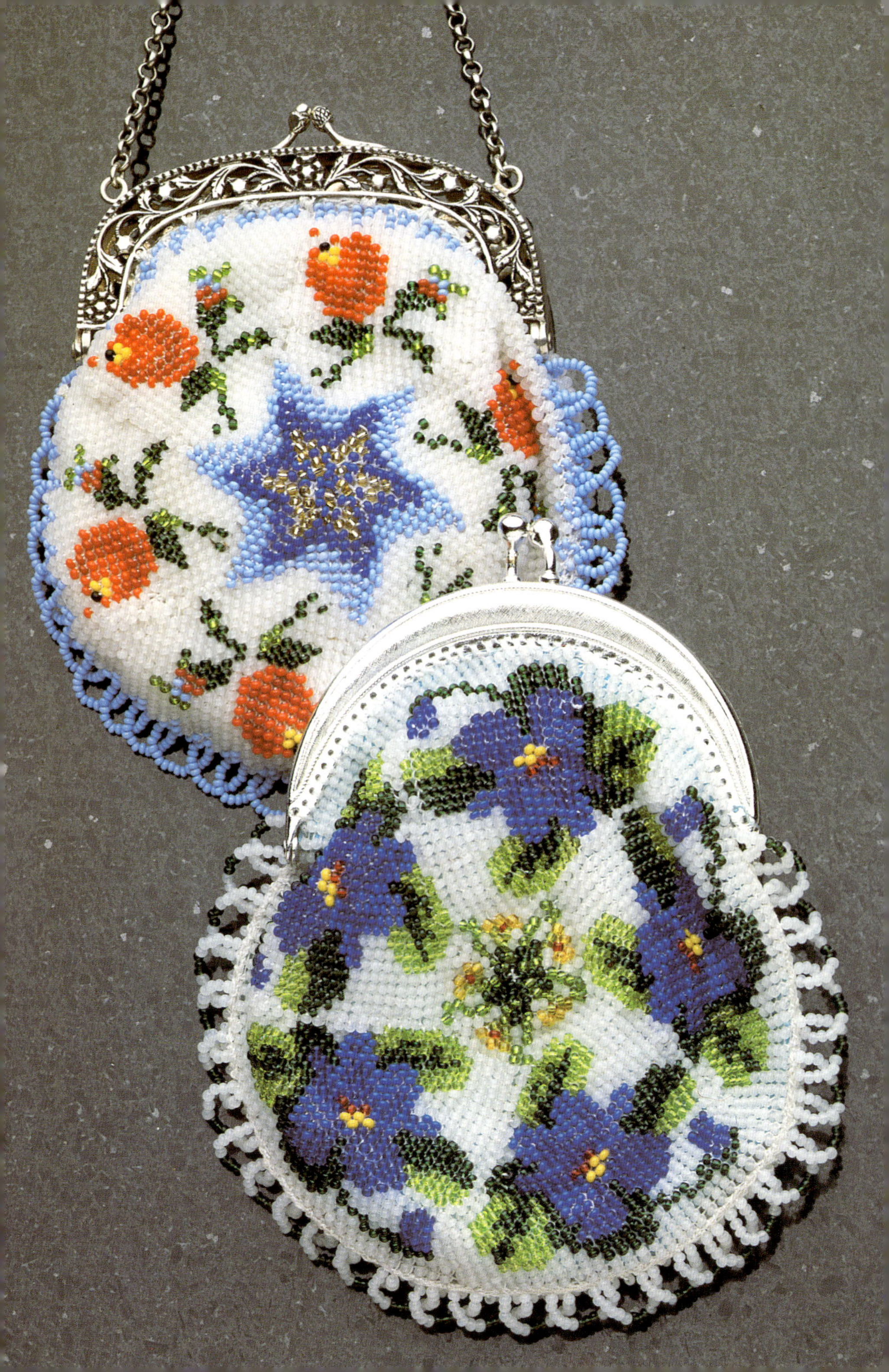

continue to B (24 beads). Thread 5 x 24 beads (each point has 24 beads). Thread each of the next 4 rows of beads 5 times also. Cast on 5 x 24 stitches = 120 stitches. Knit 2 rows moss stitch and work the next row with 5 groups of beads (A–B). This will bring you back to A. Work the next 4 rows similarly.

You will now have to thread more beads and decrease in the following rows. Decrease at the first stitch of each point, that is, the 24th stitch of the previous point is carried to the first new stitch of the next point. Repeat this 5 times. Continue knitting as described in the pattern and make the other half in the same way.

Sew the two halves together for two-thirds of the way around, leaving one-third open for the clasp.

Make sure all the points face the same way. Finish the purse by adding beaded loops around the edge as in colour plate 3.

Both the star purse and the spider purse (illustration 3) were found throughout the Netherlands. Each region had its own colour combinations and the borders around the outside varied widely. Apparently cross-stitch patterns were used for the borders. and the choice was very personal.

The star purse can be made with equilateral triangles. As a variation the triangles can be replaced with red or blue flowers. Check that the number of stitches in the pattern coincides with the number of stitches required to make the flowers, decreasing or increasing stitches as necessary. When decreasing make sure that the decreases are in line with the previous row. The last stitches left in the middle can be placed on a thread and pulled tight.

Translucent white beads are usually used for the background. For a different effect they can be dyed with black tea.

The star purses can also be started from the middle, which means that instead of decreasing, the stitches are increased. In

<**Colour plate 3** *Two star purses with flowers and violets (see diagrams 7b and 7c)*

theory the first method is stronger and more effective.

The next examples will now be easier to make. It is usually best to start working from the bottom, to build up the pattern. As the purses are usually the same on both sides, each row is made twice. At the bottom you will need to decrease on an angle. This can be done by dividing the work in two and starting each row from the same side or knitting the returning row in purl. Make sure when you are knitting that the beads are placed correctly.

Purl knitting

To knit the top of the purse the work is divided into two pieces. To achieve the stocking [stockinette] stitch effect that you get from knitting in the round (in this case twisted knit), you will need to knit one row and purl one row (in this case twisted purl). Inexperienced knitters may find it difficult to get an even finish when the beads have to be included in the purl rows. The beads must be visible on the right (knit) side of the work, thus it is easier to push the stitches back to the end of the needle and, using a new thread, knit the next row. This can be done if you are using double-pointed knitting needles.

The more experienced knitter can work the return row in purl. Push the point of the right needle into the back of the stitch, yarn over needle, making sure bead is in front of the needle. With the thumb of the left hand push the bead to the front of the work before completing the stitch. Complete the stitch, making sure the bead does not slip to the back.

When the work is divided into two pieces use a crochet hook for the first row and crochet half chains [slip stitches] until the second row. You could make 4 or 5 rows this way. Continue in stocking [stockinette] stitch until the work is long enough to fit the side of the clasp.

Casting off

Casting off must be done very loosely to allow enough room to attach the clasp. Usually the top [of the old purses] was not decreased, but attached straight to the clasp. This created a pleat at the hinge and caused tension in the centre of the knitting. Most of the old purses tended to break at that point. To prevent this, you could fix a small piece of lining fabric, cut diagonally, to the clasp. When the clasp is opened it rubs against the lining fabric, preventing damage to the beads.

Stretching

Because most of the knitting is done in a twisted knit stitch the finished purses tend to twist. To counteract this they can be stretched, done by dipping the purse quickly in hot water and then pinning it onto a piece of chipboard (or polystyrene foam). Make a paper pattern of the correct shape and fix it to the board before pinning out the wet purse. Leave to dry into shape.
The purse could also be sprayed with liquid starch to keep its shape.
To keep the beaded surface smooth the inside of the purse could be lined with iron-on Vilene [fusible interfacing]. This is not strictly necessary, but it can give a very good effect.

Lining the bag and attaching the clasp

The purses of earlier times were usually lined with a piece of chamois leather, which was easily washable. You could use chamois if you wish, but a piece of strong lining fabric is just as serviceable.
To make the lining, cut a pattern using the knitted work as model. Use a compass to draw the lining pattern for a round purse. Cut the lining approximately 1 cm (5/8") larger all around and stitch around. Leave the top slightly wider.
For a clasp with three parts cut the pattern three times, making the piece for the middle slightly longer so a seam can be made in it.
Nick the seam of the lining at regular intervals to fit as shown in illustration 8. Fold in the top of the lining and the top of the purse and sew them together.
Attach the completed purse to the clasp at both ends and the centre of the clasp with small stitches. The rest of the purse is fitted evenly to the clasp.
Purses made of open crochet work should have a double lining to hide the seams of the lining.

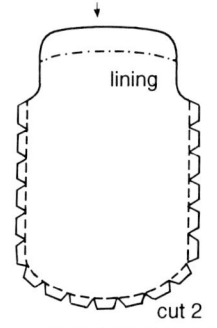

cut 2
cut 3 if clasp has centre piece

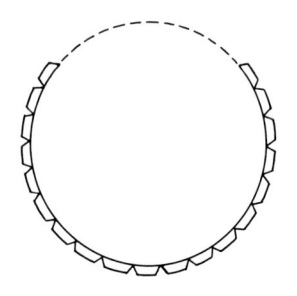

Illustration 8 *Pattern for lining, showing how to cut the seam*

3. Patterns

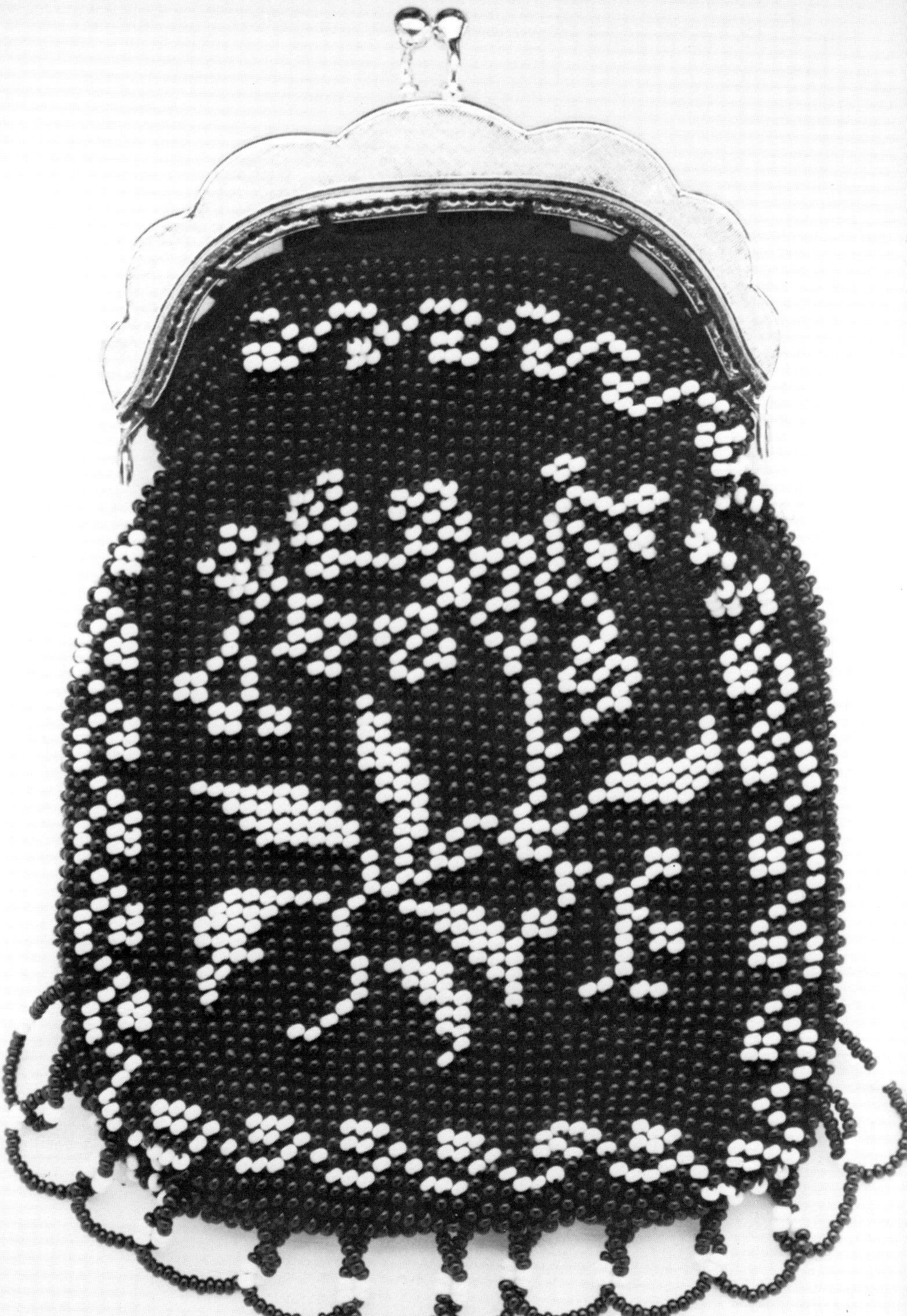

Black and white purse: Wouterswoude

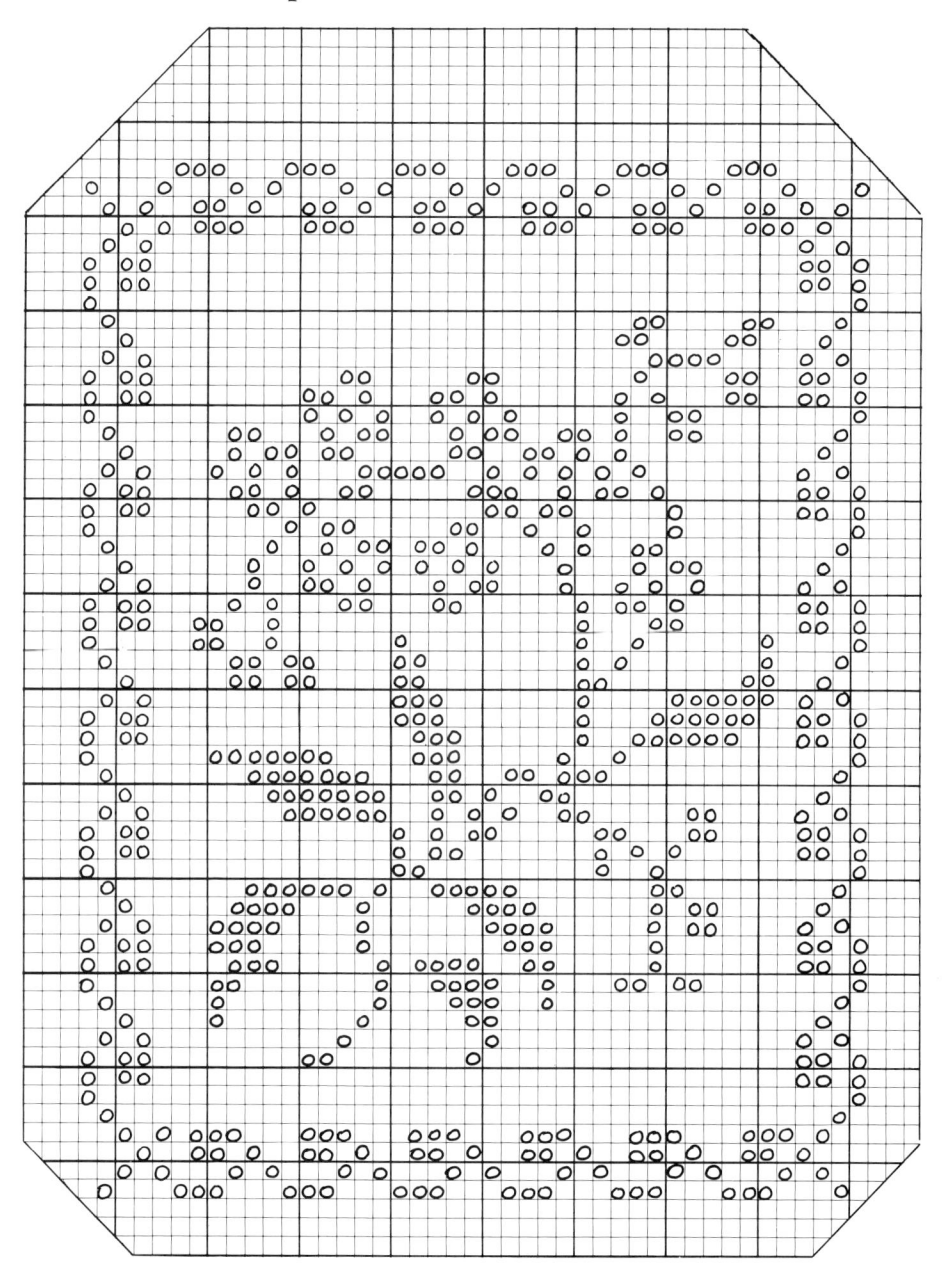

9a Pattern for black and white purse from Wouterswoude (forest of the hunters)

< 9 Black and white purse from Wouterswoude. These black and white purses were also used as mourning purses. They can of course be made in any colour

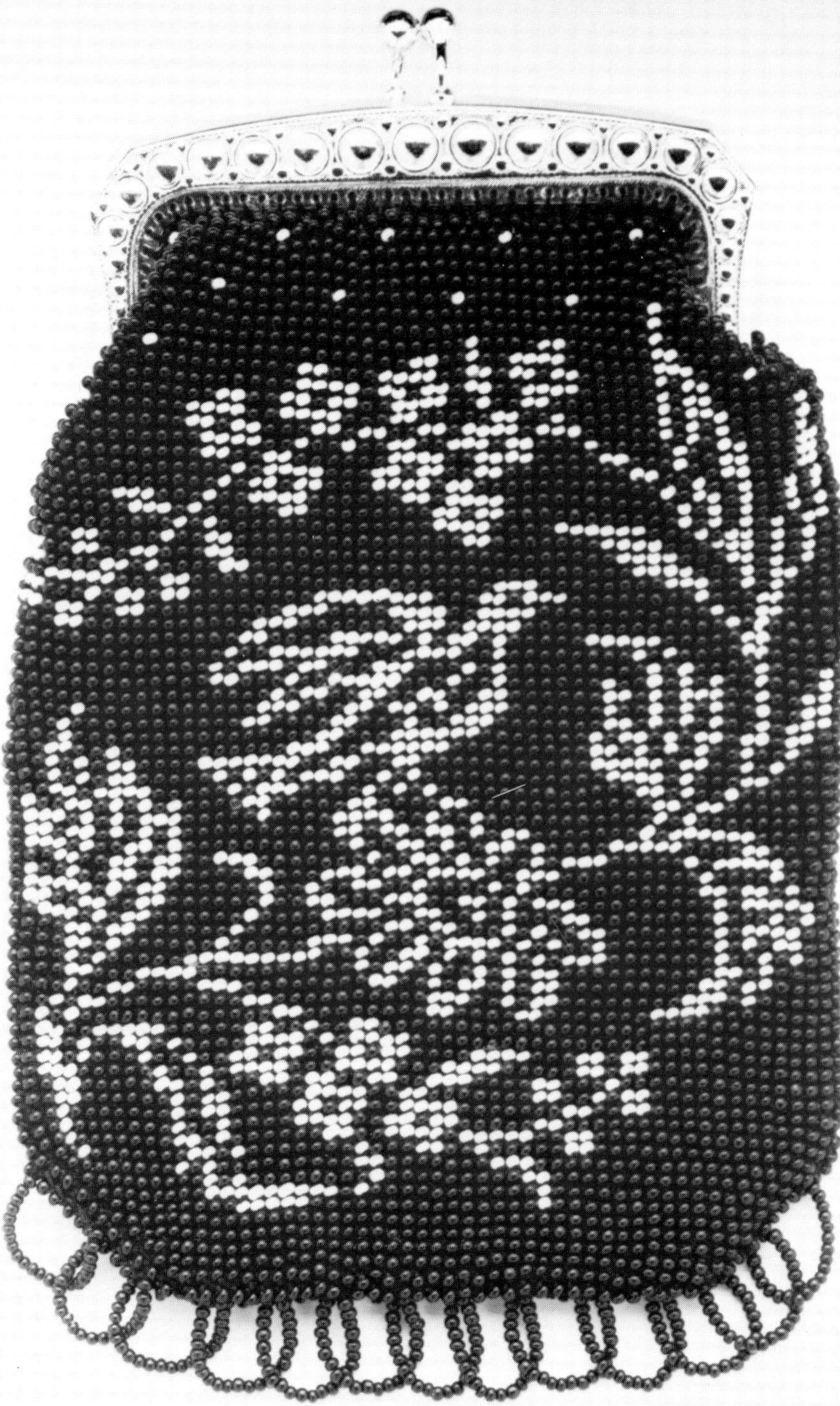

Black and white purse: Bird on a branch

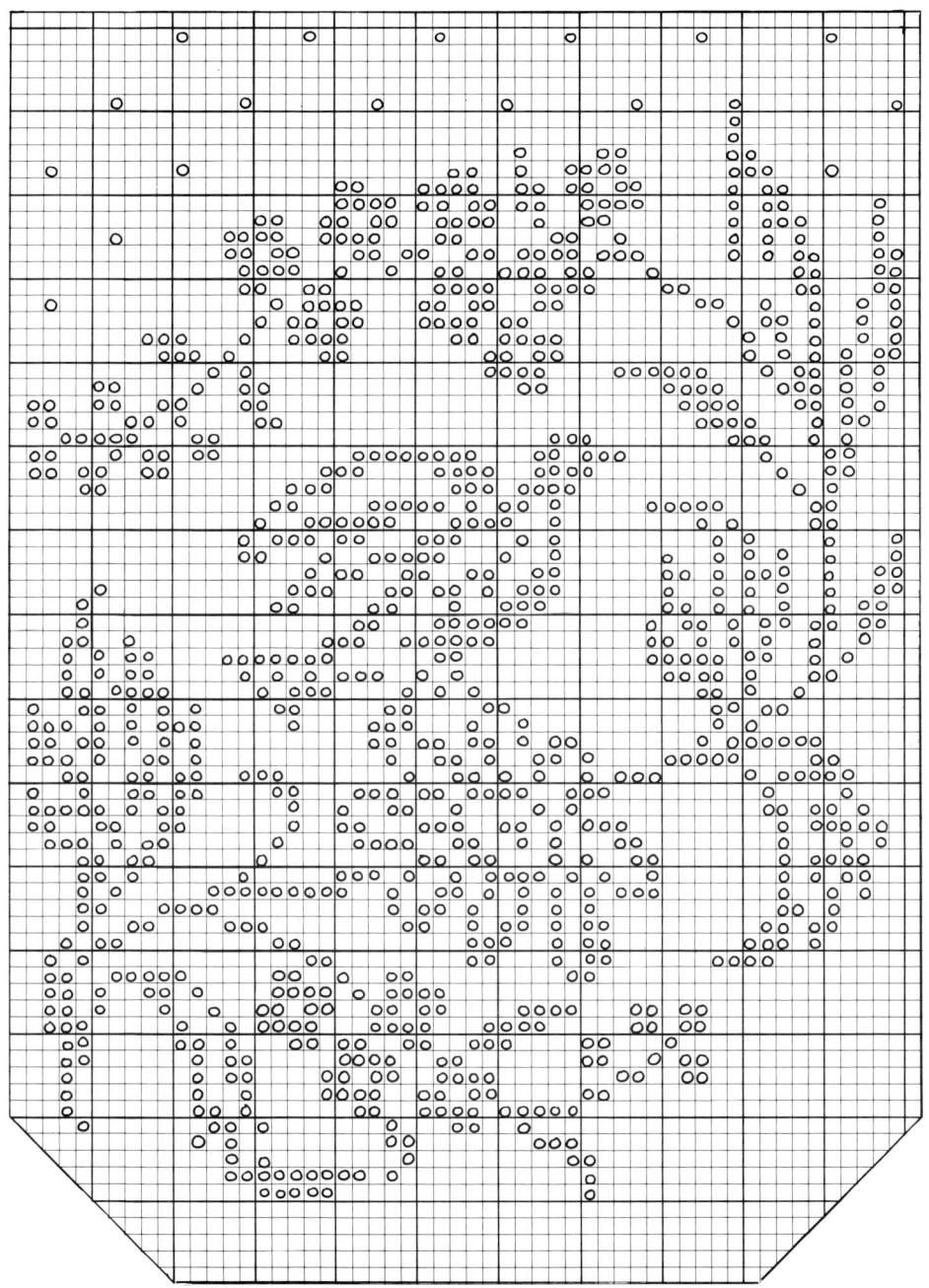

< 10 *Black and white purse: Bird on a branch*   ^ 10 *Pattern for Bird on a branch*

Leeuwarden (Lion's heart)

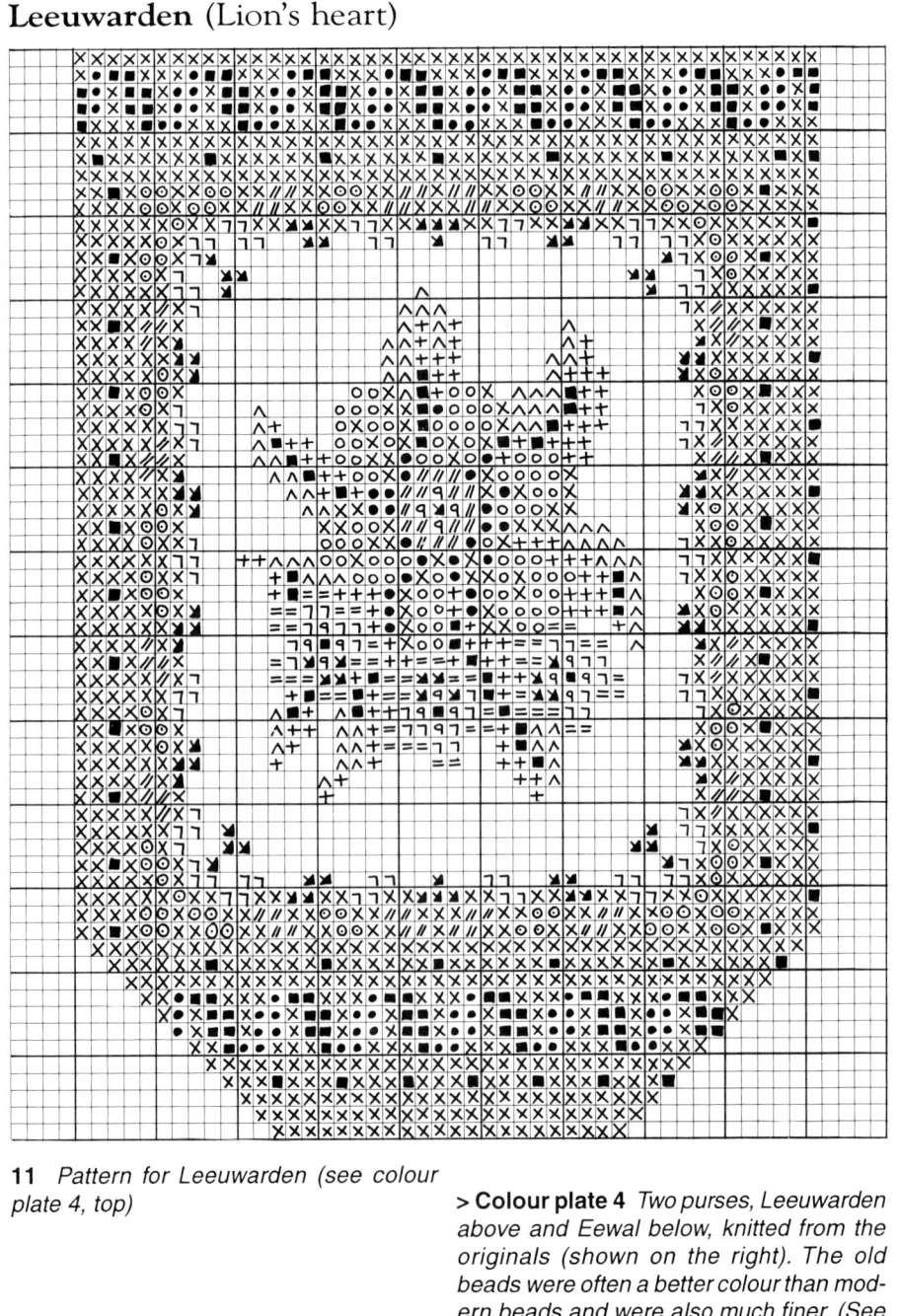

11 Pattern for Leeuwarden (see colour plate 4, top)

> **Colour plate 4** Two purses, Leeuwarden above and Eewal below, knitted from the originals (shown on the right). The old beads were often a better colour than modern beads and were also much finer. (See also pattern diagrams 11 and 12)

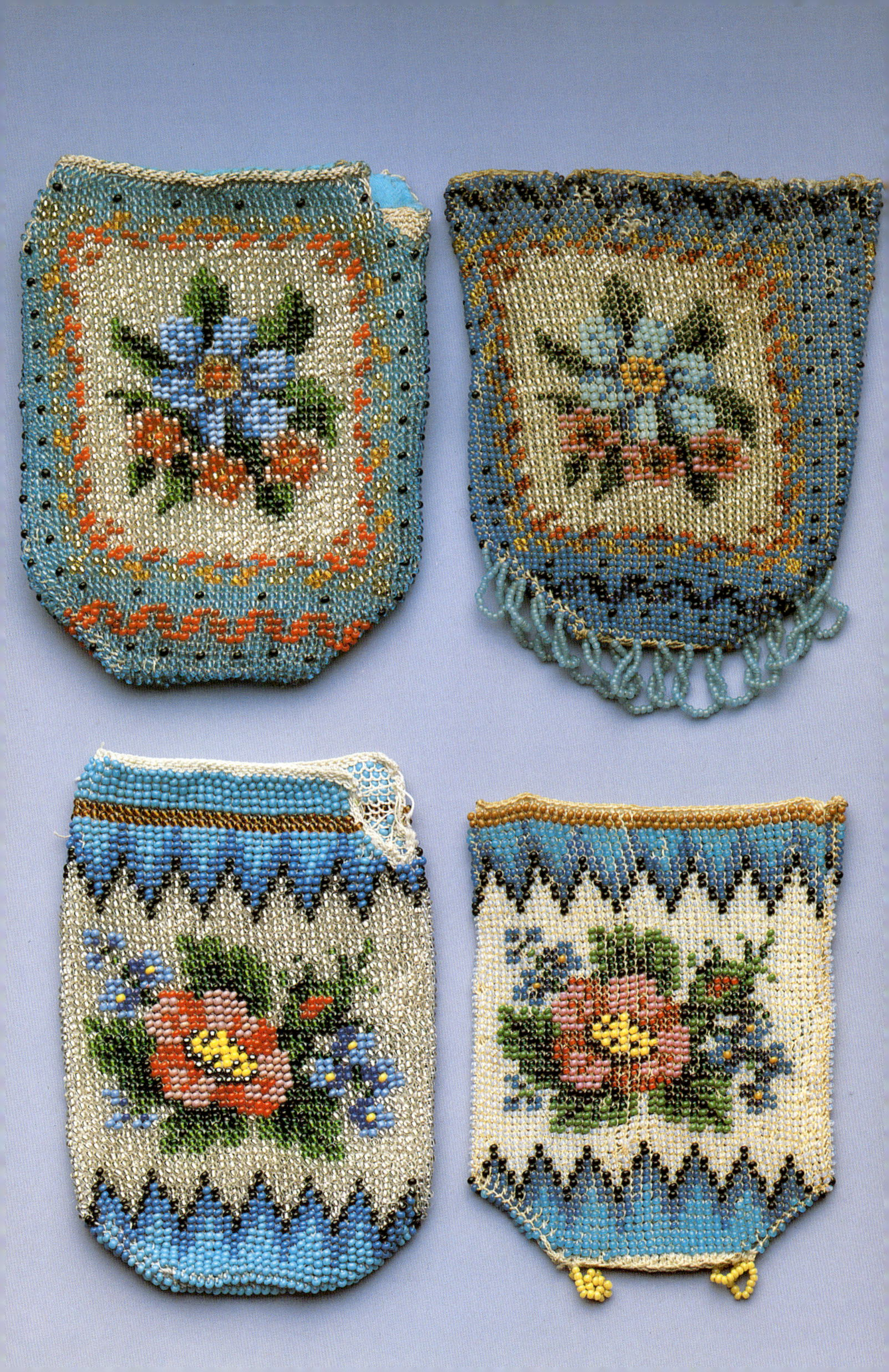

Eewal (Weir on the lake)

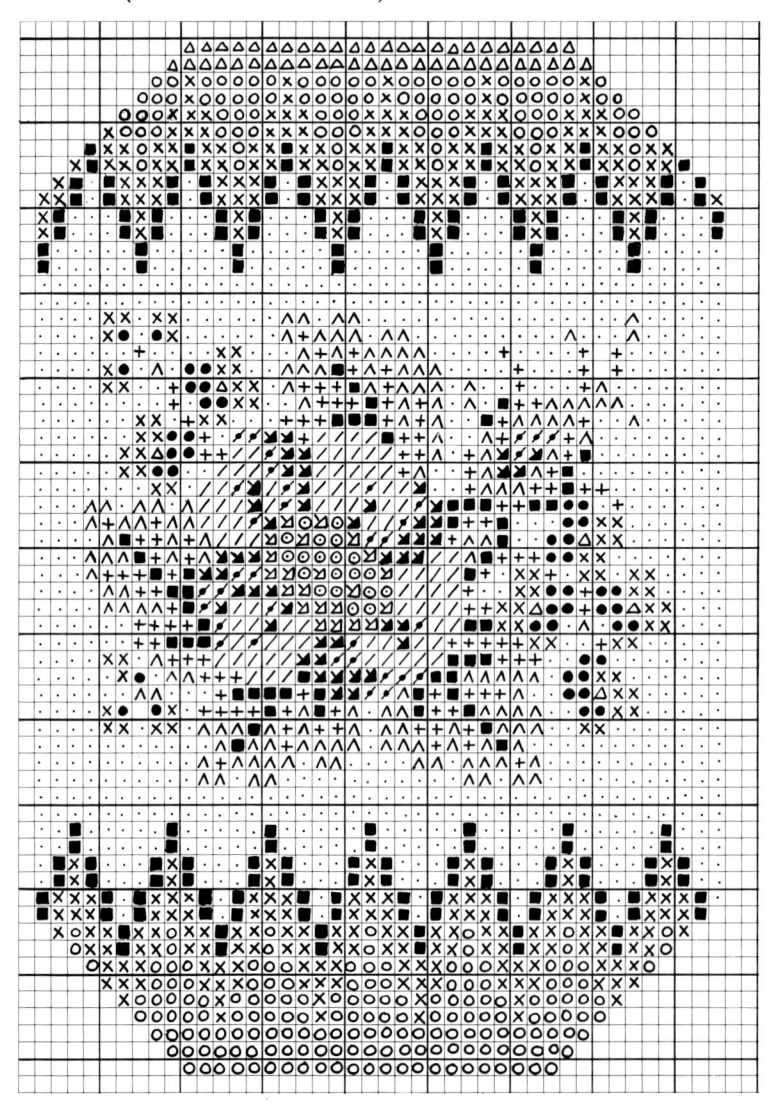

12 Pattern for Eewal (see colour plate 4)

> **Colour plate 5** Two beautiful old purses, Oostermeer above and Rose with orange flower below (see pattern diagrams 13 and 14)

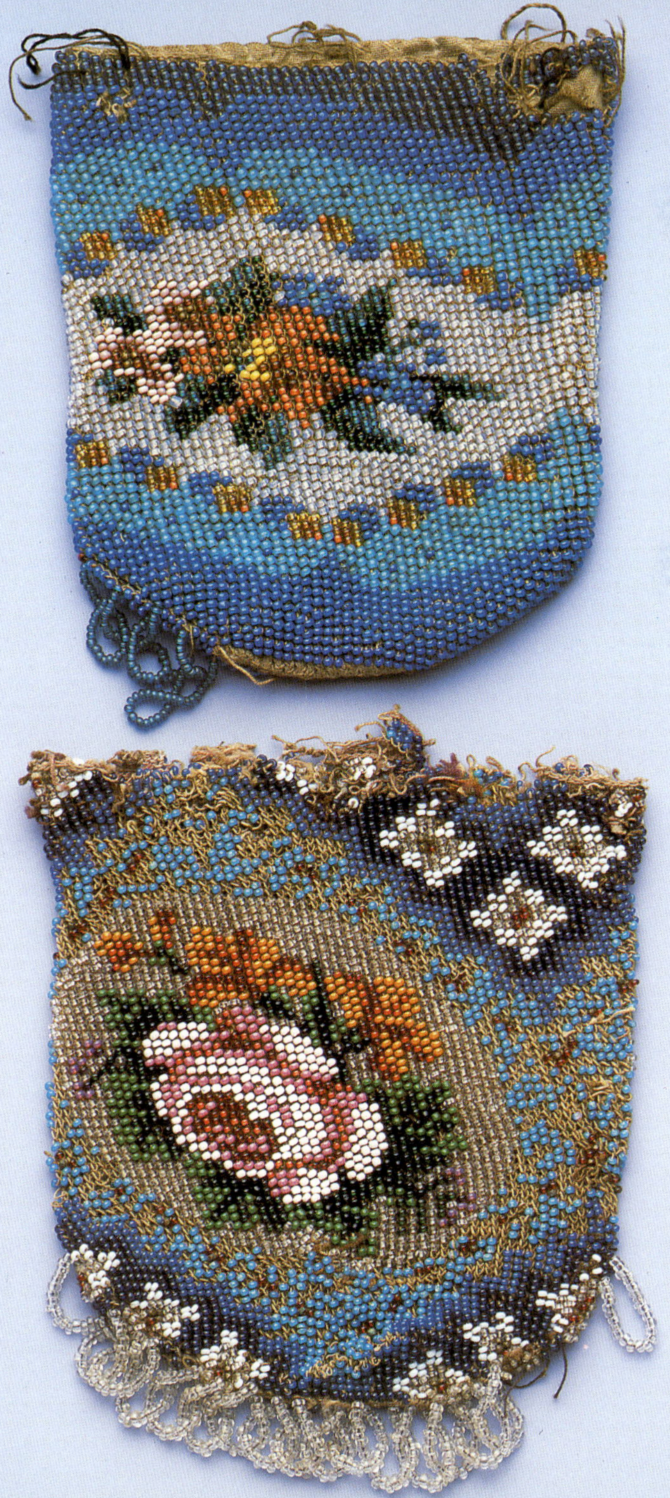

Oostermeer (Eastern lake)

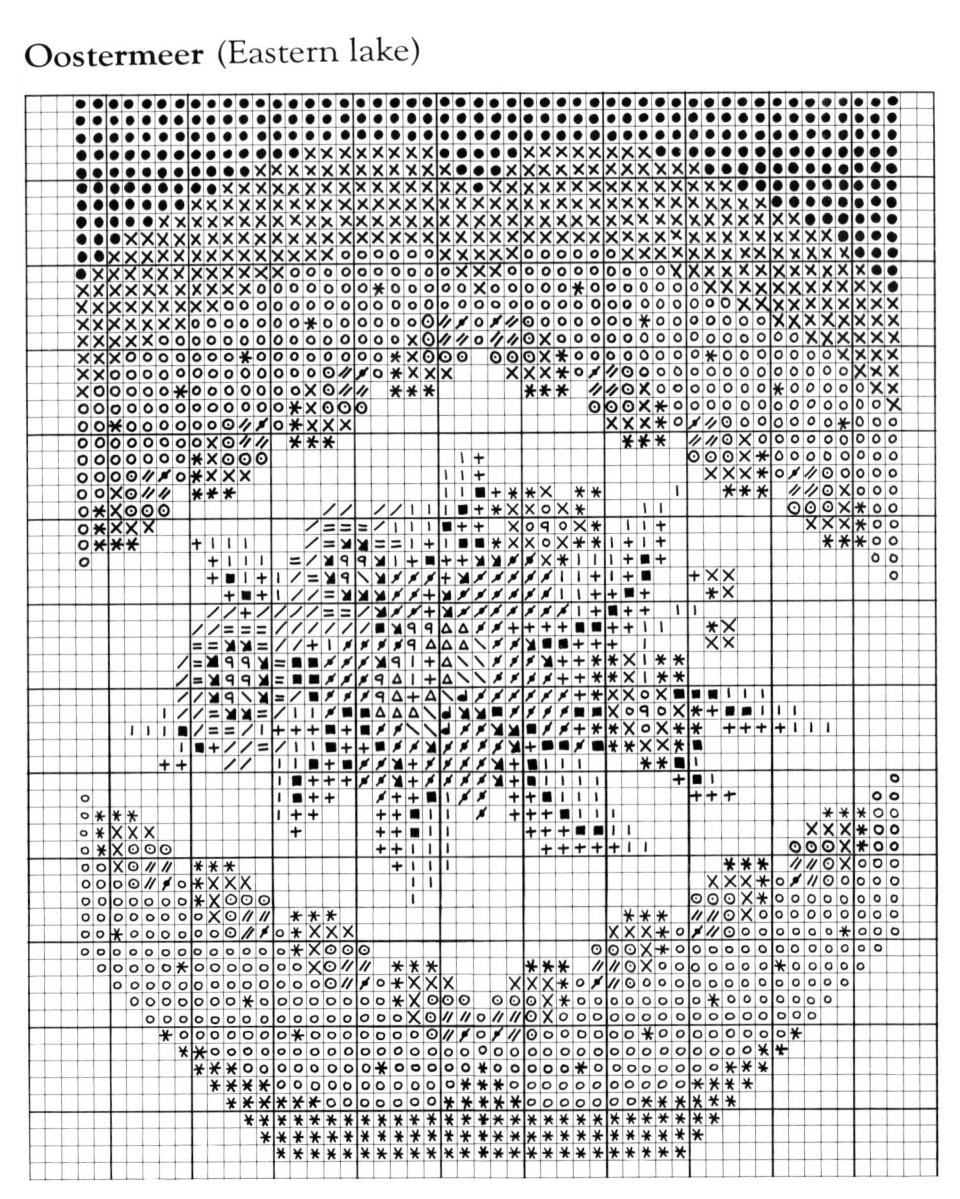

13 *Pattern for Oostermeer (see colour plate 5)*

Rose with orange flower

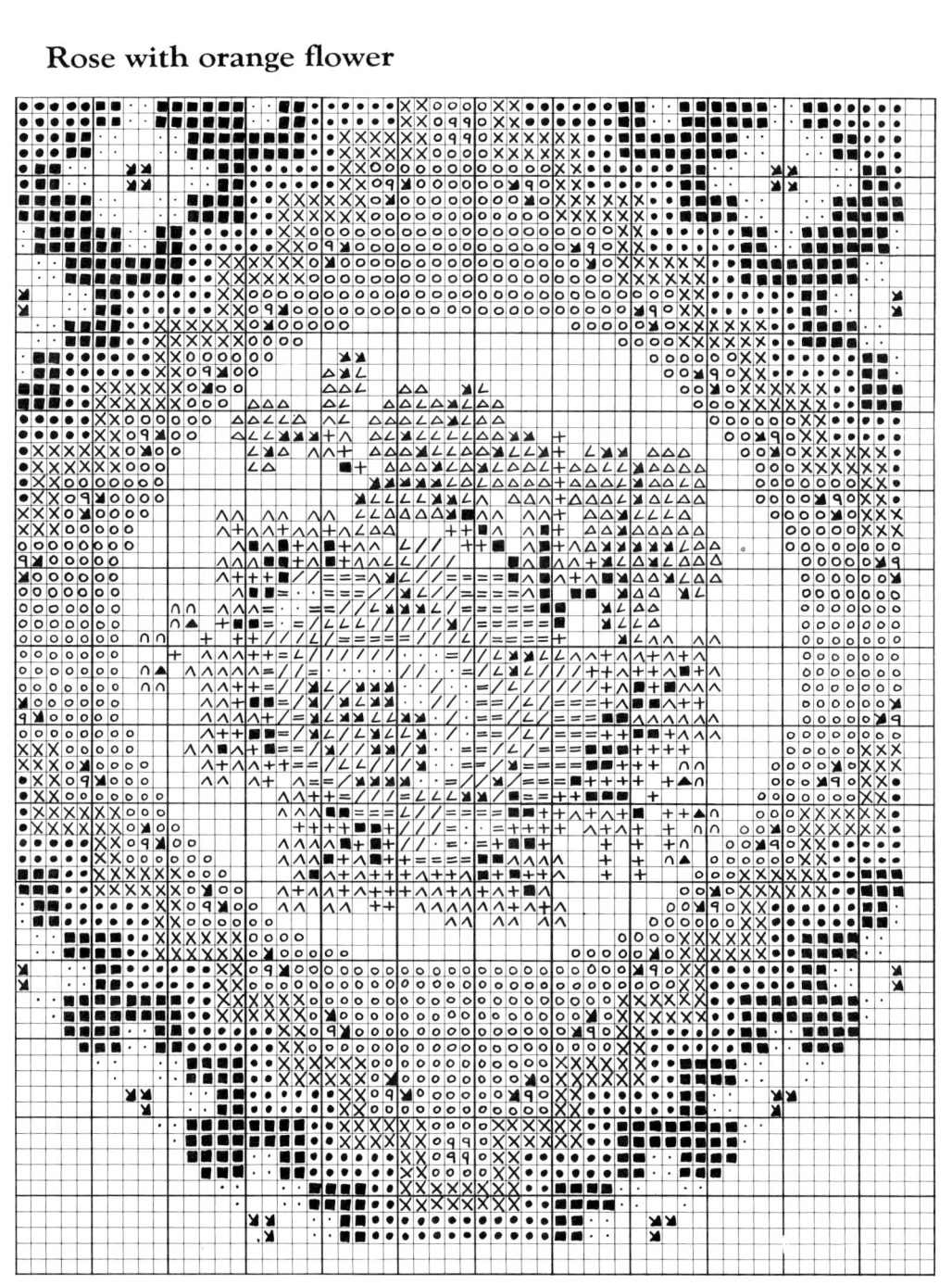

^ 14 *Pattern for Rose with orange flower (see colour plate 5)*

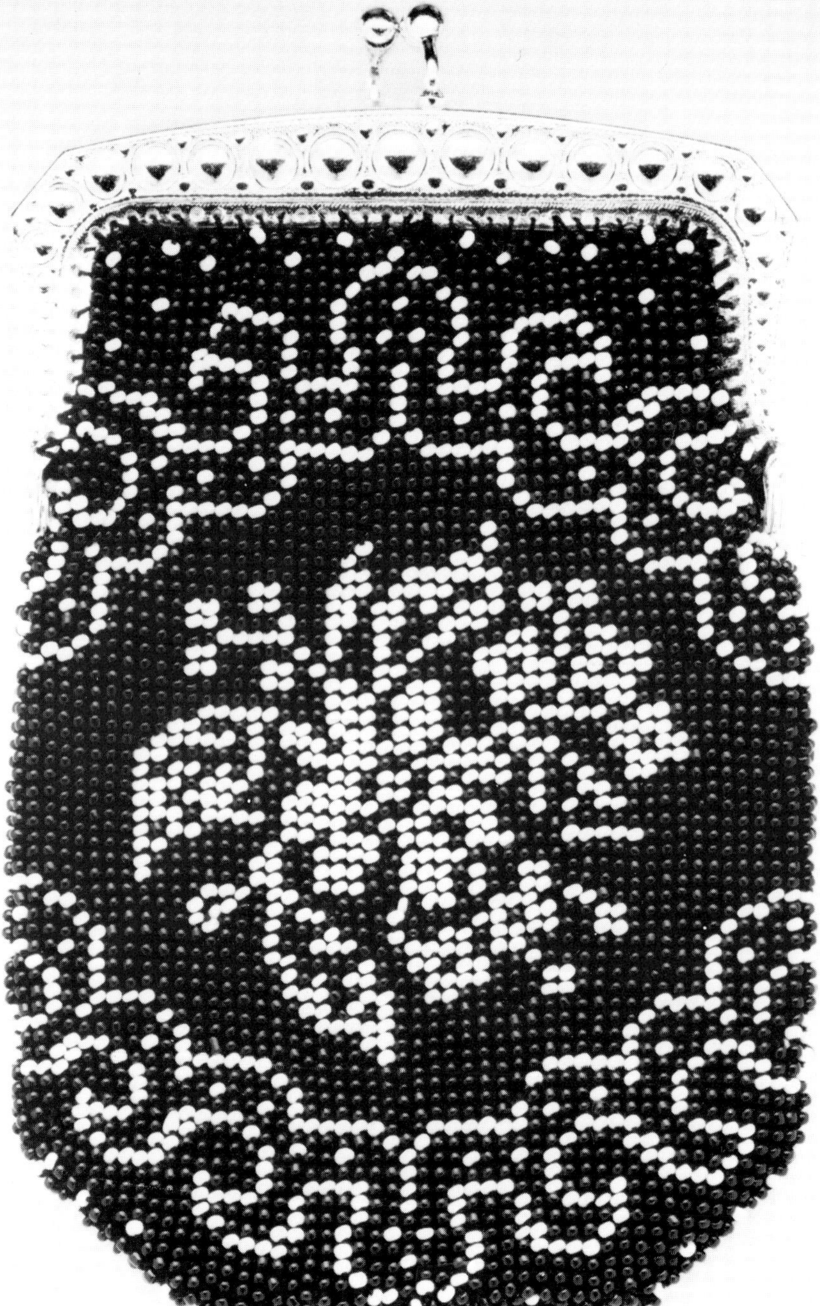

Black and white purse: Flower with border

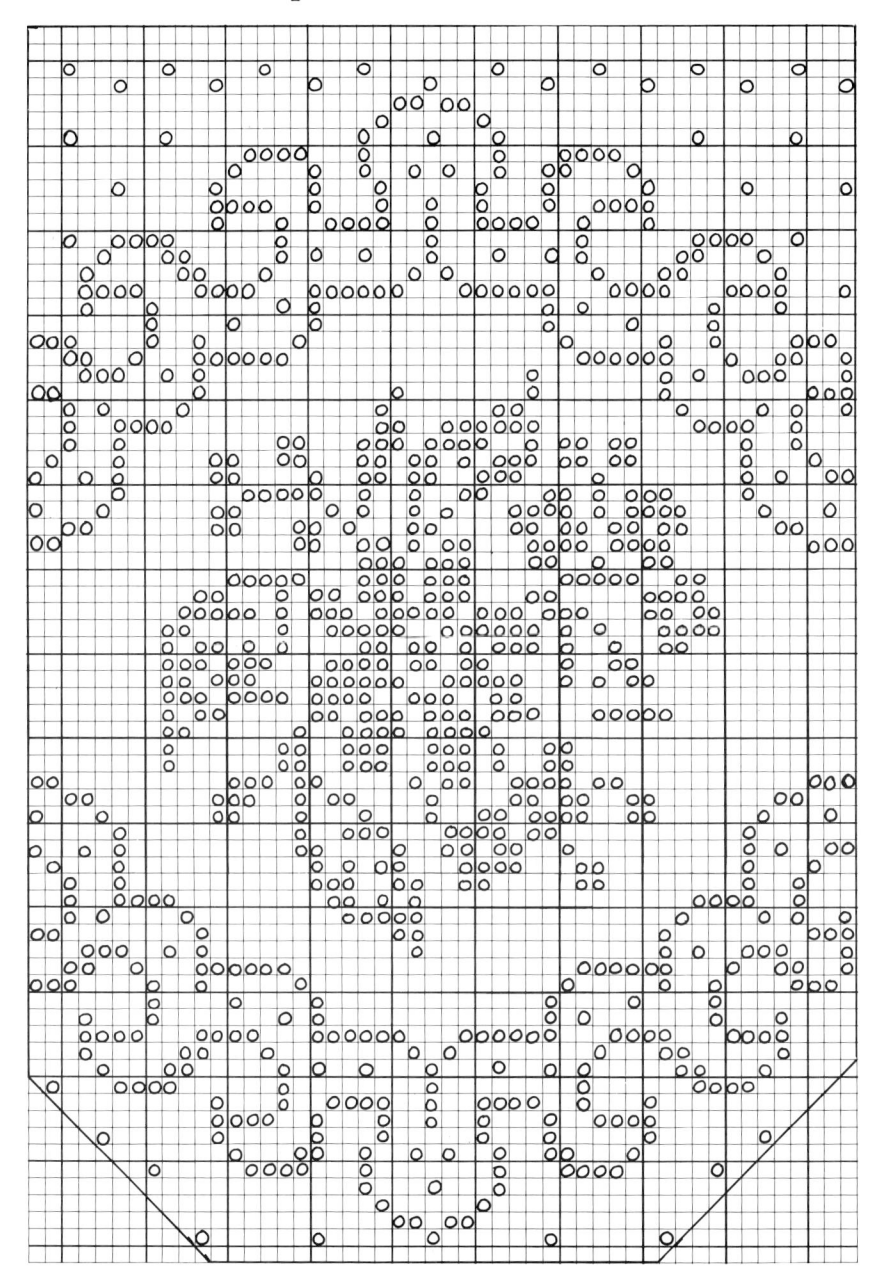

< **15** Black and white purse: Flower with border

^ **15a** Pattern for black and white purse: Flower with border

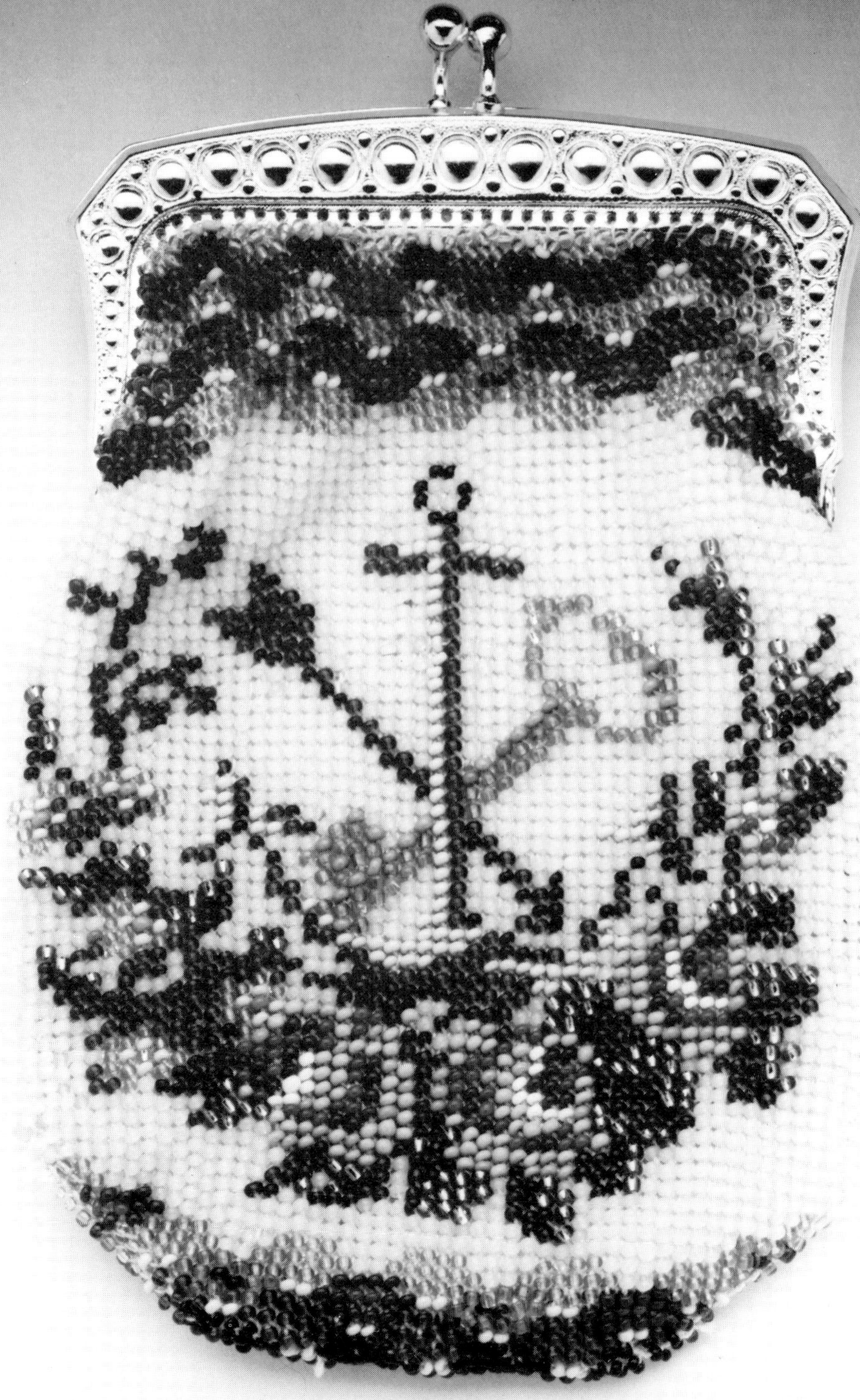

Faith, hope and charity

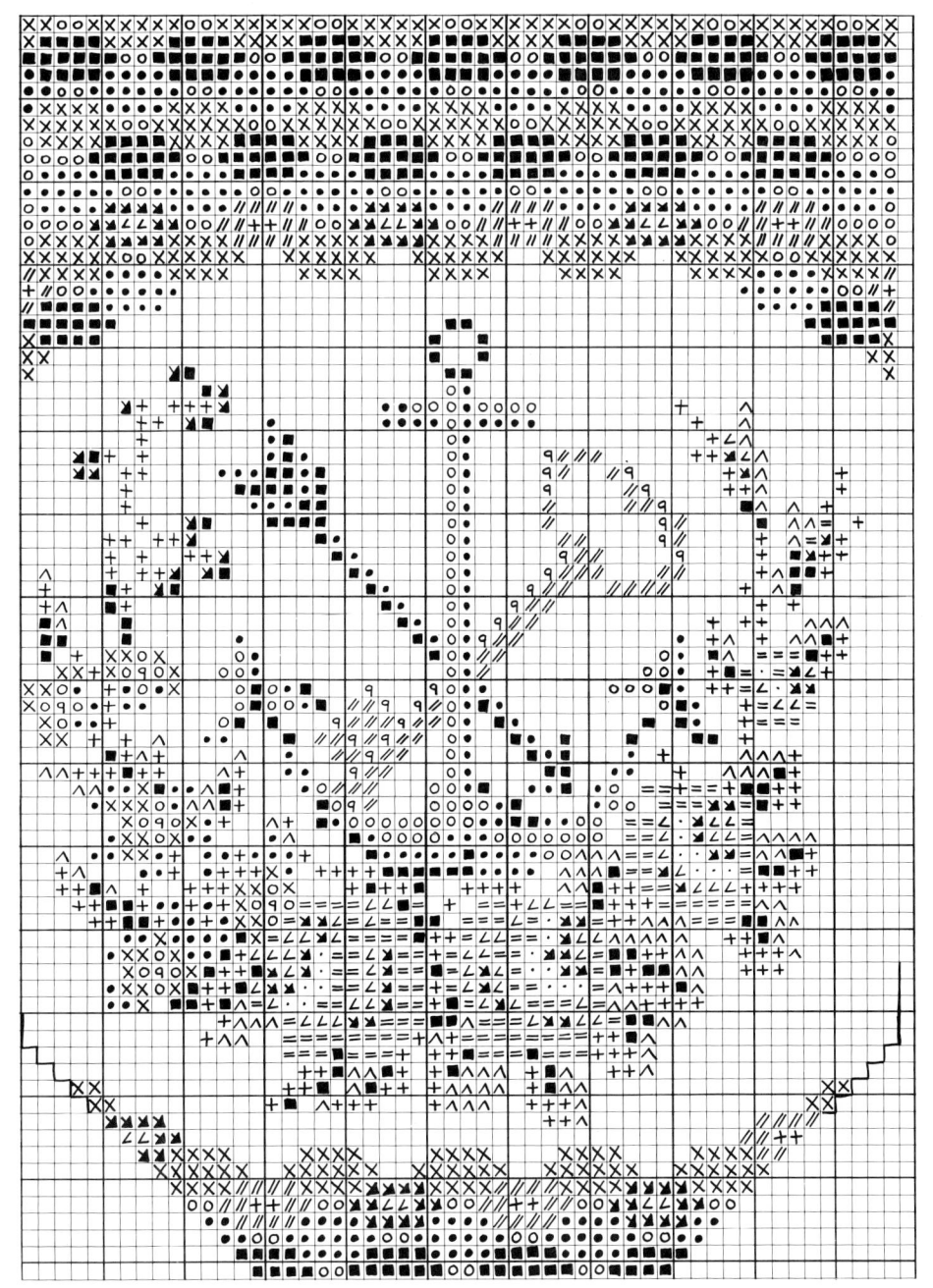

<16 Faith, hope and charity: Christian symbols were often used in purses

^16a Pattern for Faith, hope and charity

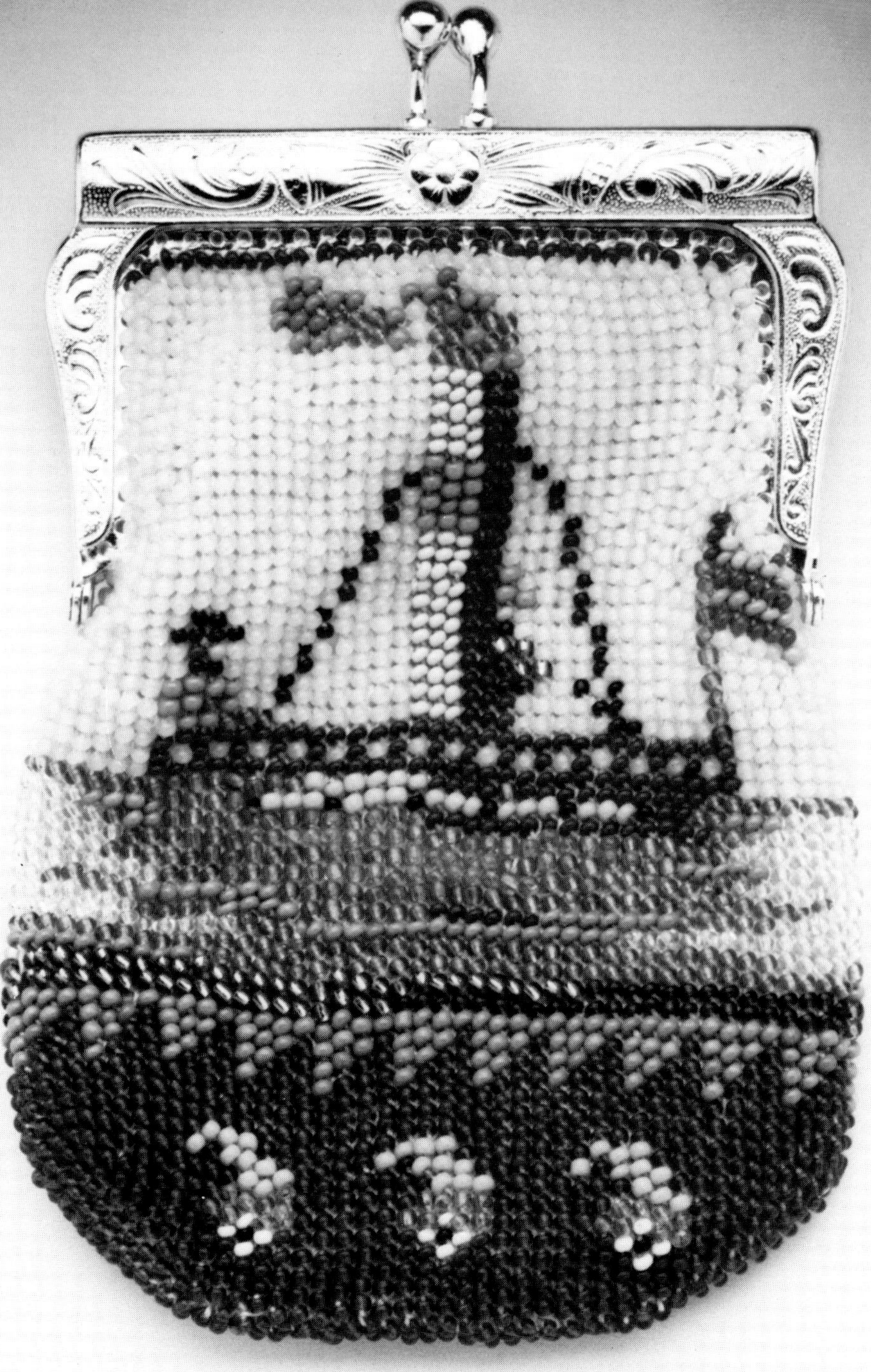

Wieringen (from Lake Wier)

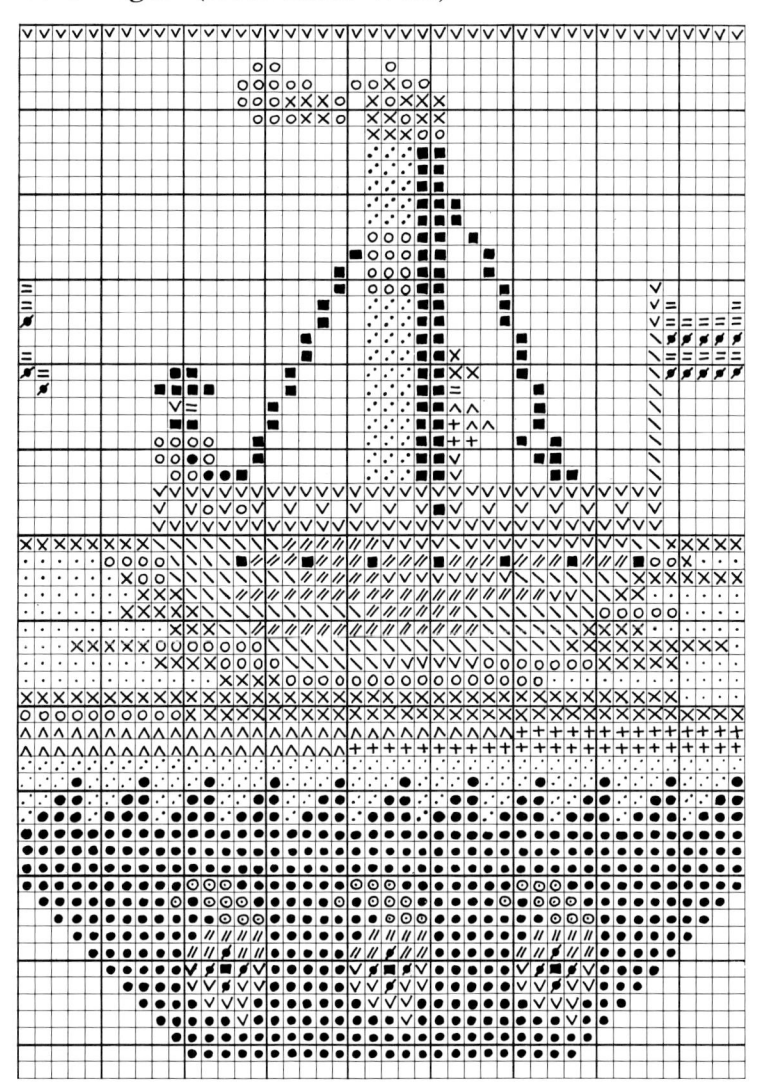

<17 *Wieringen. This purse has a lot of blue shades in it. Blue was very popular as it was thought that the colour gave protection. The people of Wieringen lived mainly as fishermen and used fishing motifs for their purses. The boats were depicted with little style and did not look like real fishing boats. Here it looks as though the wind is blowing from both sides, something also seen on old tiles*

17a *Pattern for Wieringen*

41

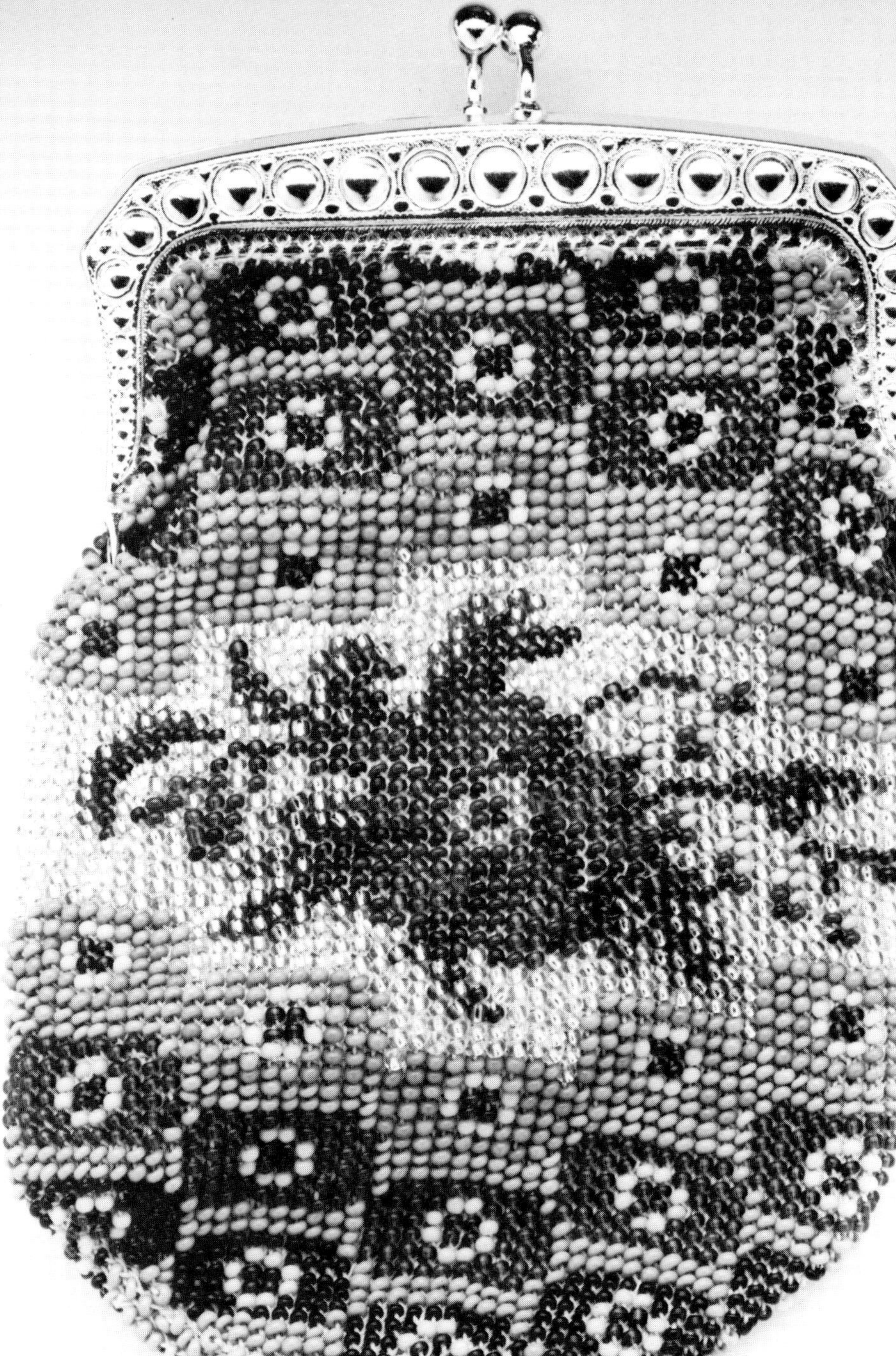

Crayfish

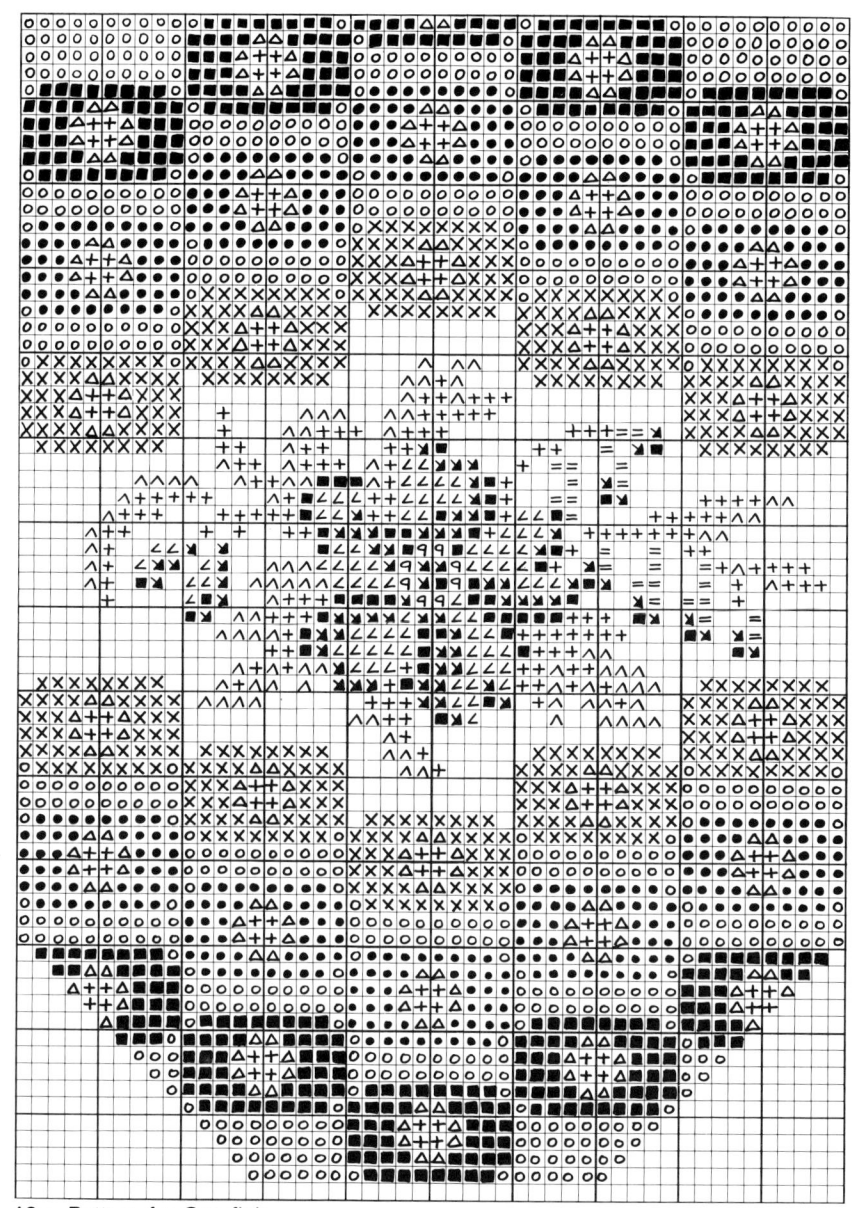

18a Pattern for Crayfish

<18 Crayfish

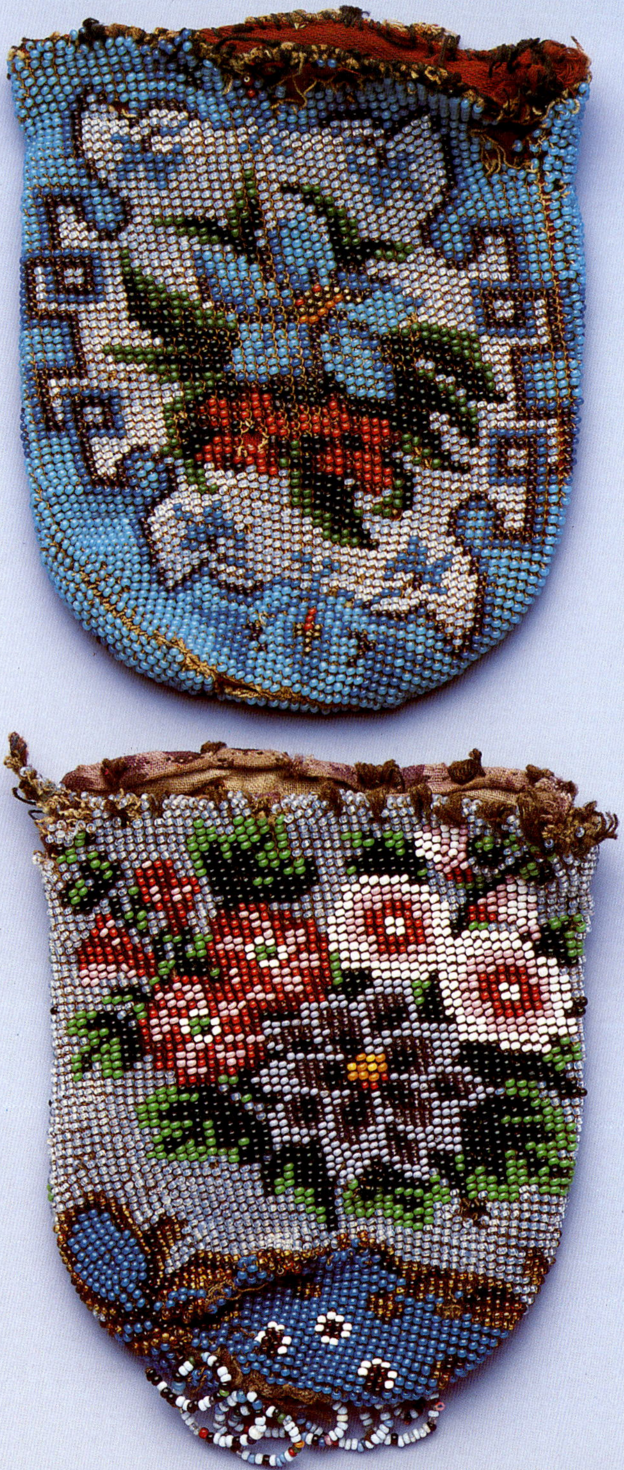

Blue flower

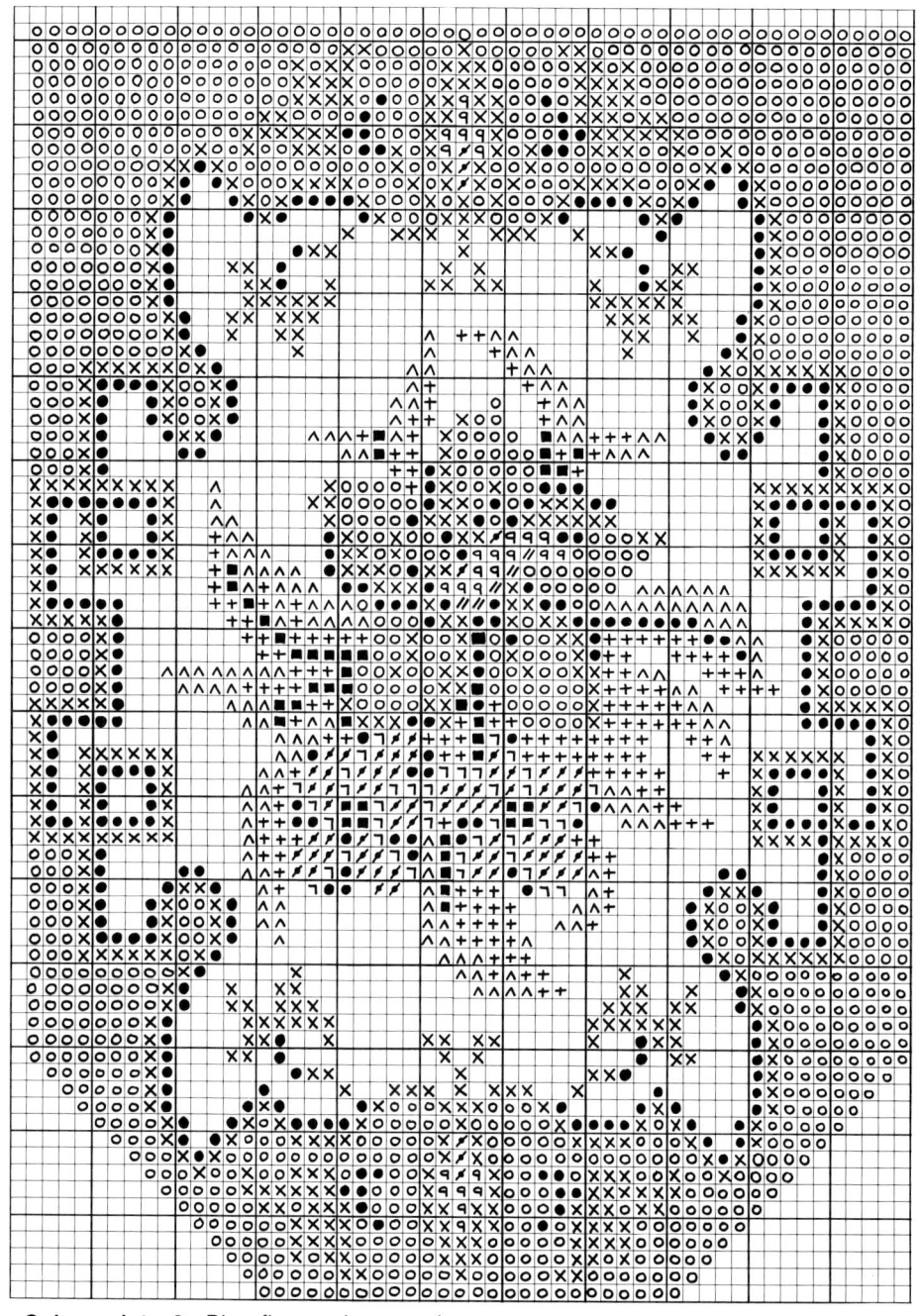

<Colour plate 6 *Blue flower above and Purple dahlia below (see pattern diagrams 19 and 20)*

^ 19 *Pattern for Blue flower (see colour plate 6)*

Purple dahlia

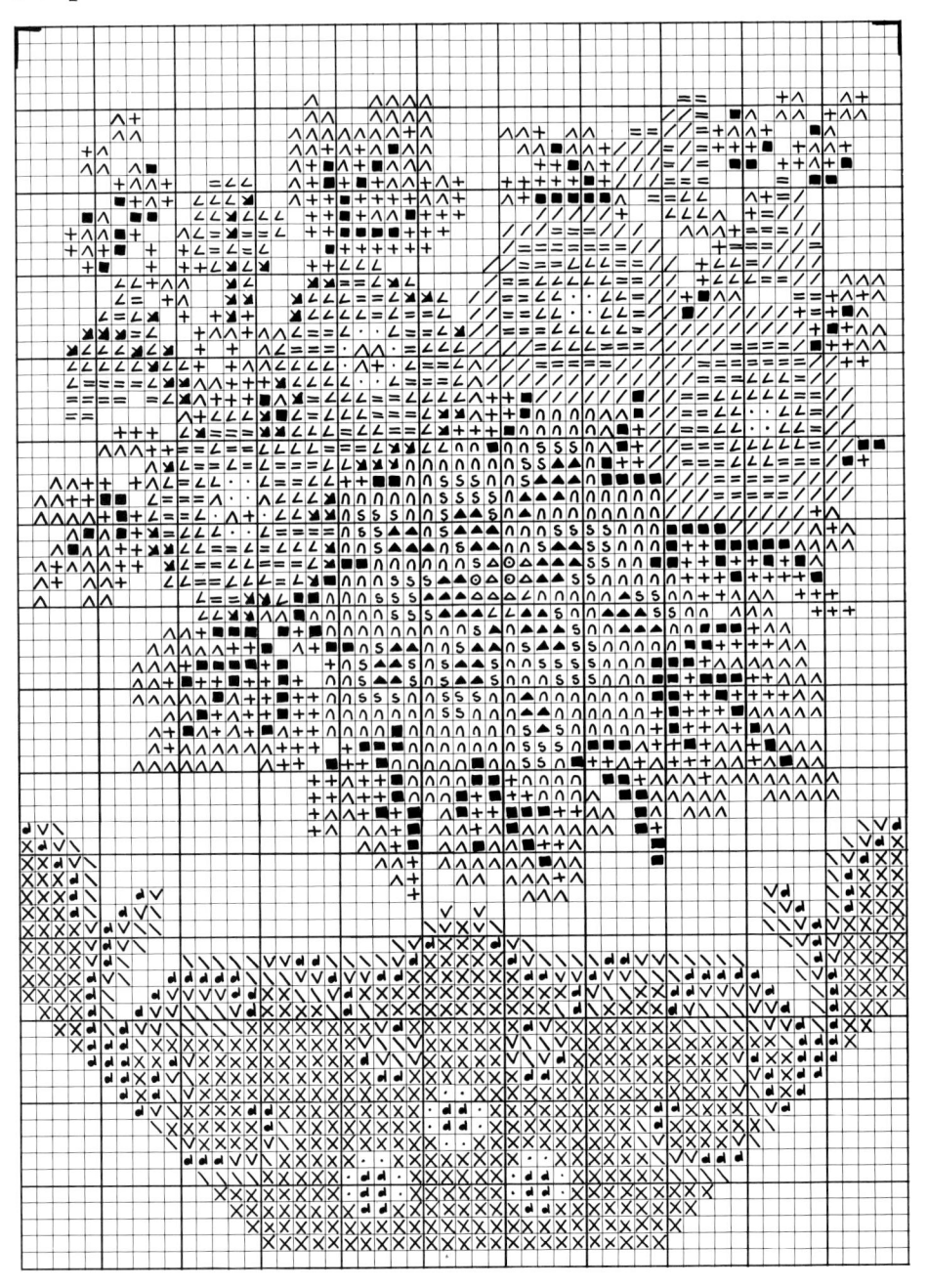

20 *Pattern for Purple dahlia (see colour plate 6)*

>**21** *Pattern for The bird (see illustration page 2)*

The bird

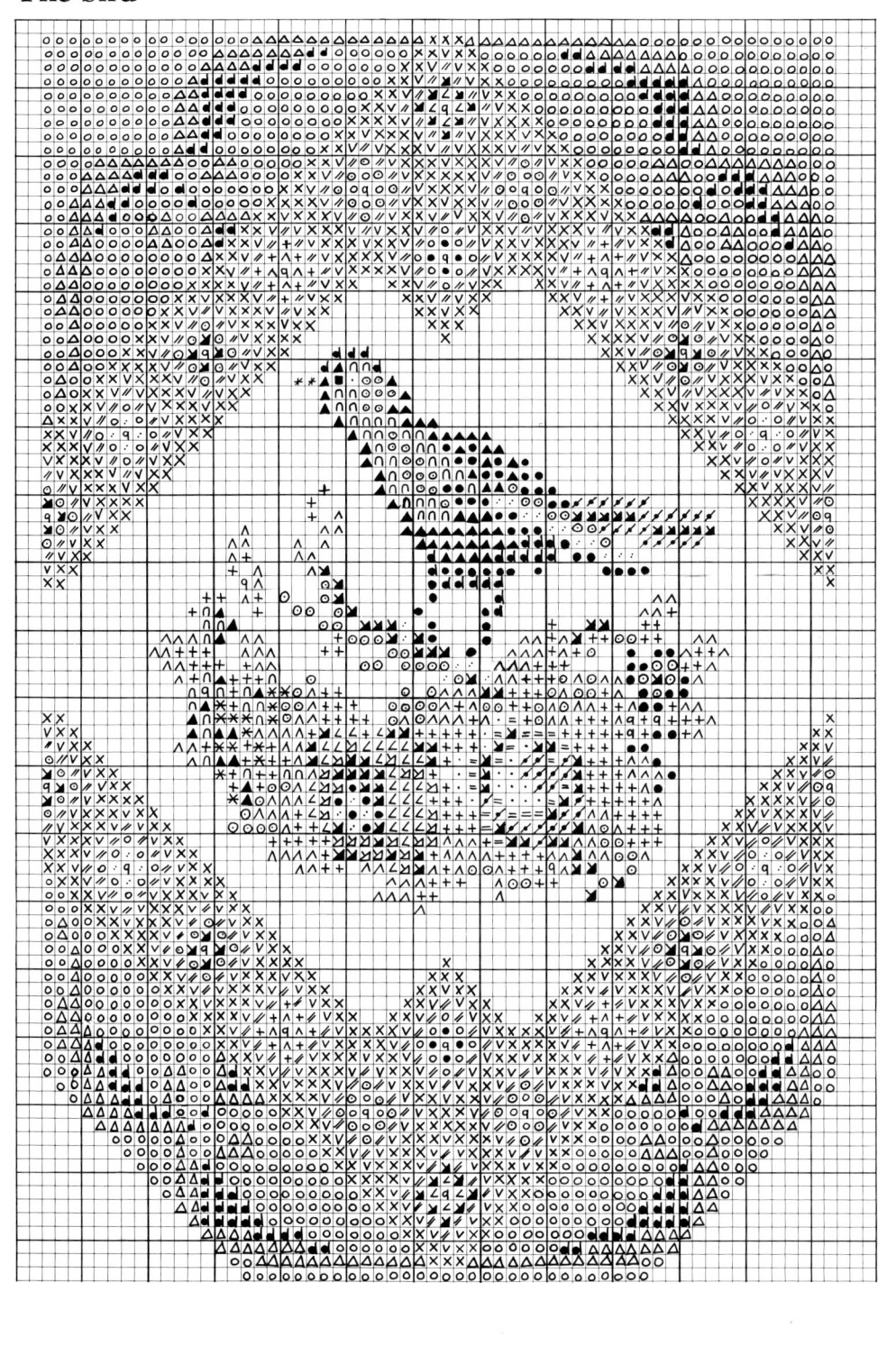

Glasses case

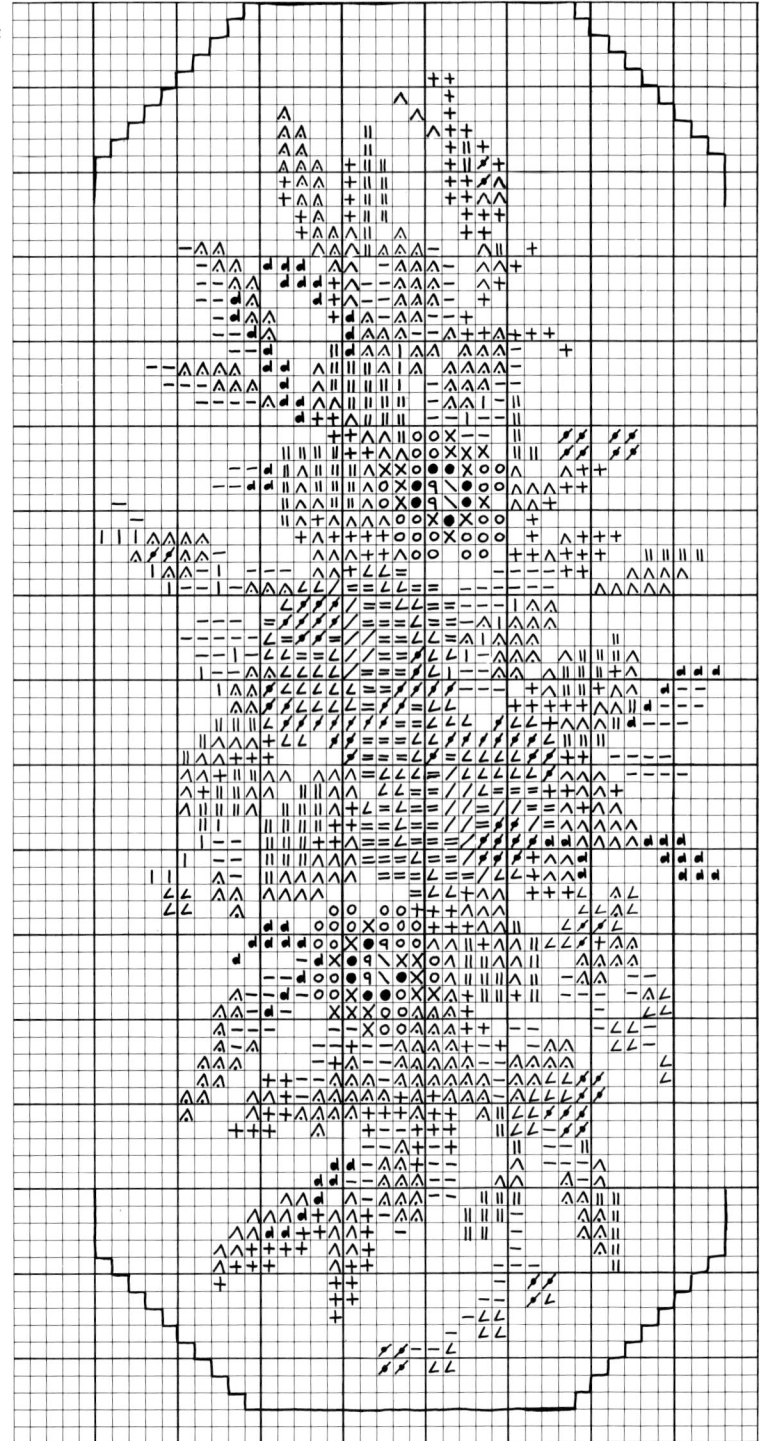

22 Pattern for Glasses case (see colour plate 7)

> **Colour plate 7** Glasses case (see pattern diagram 22)

48

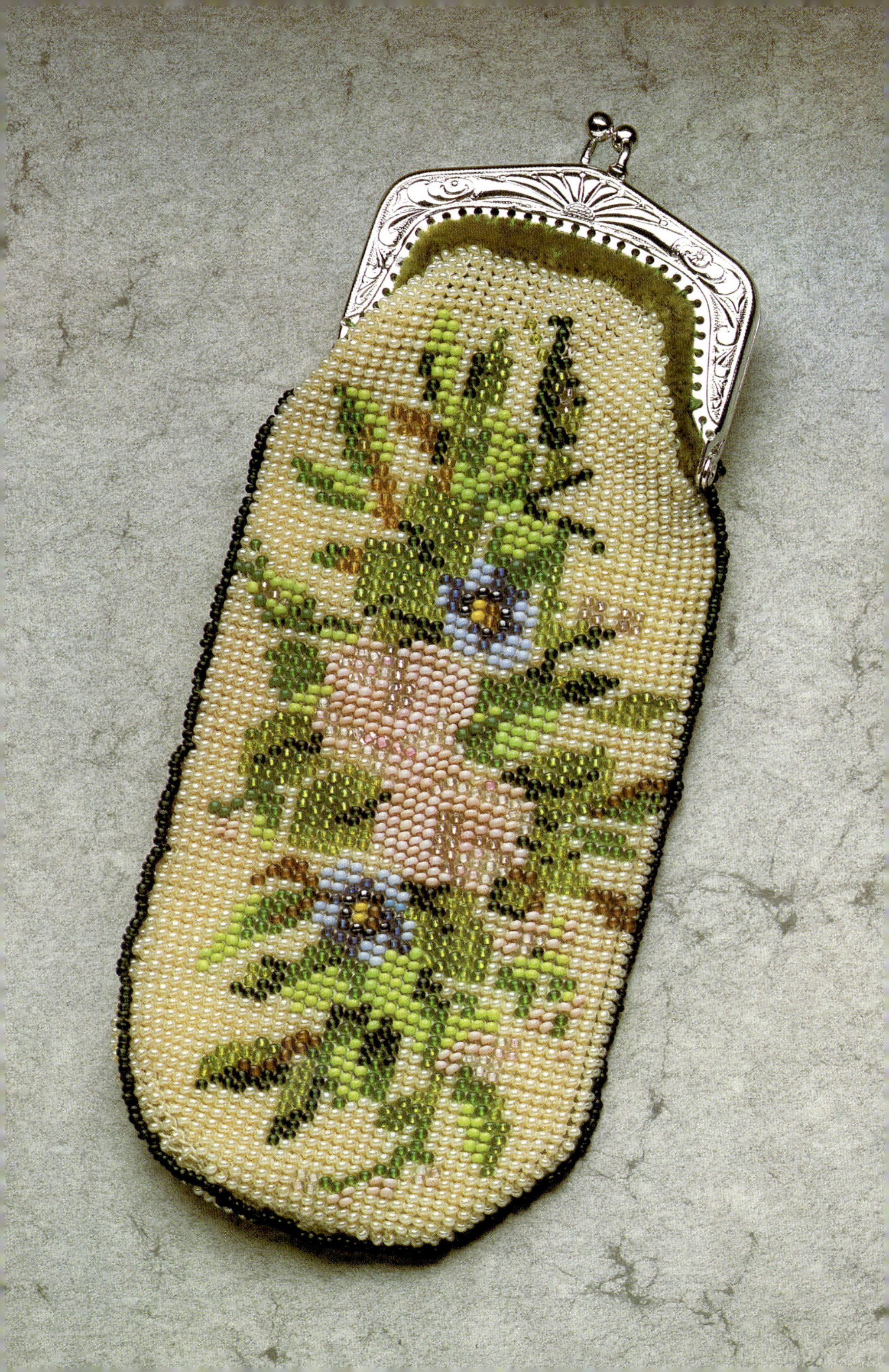

Nel

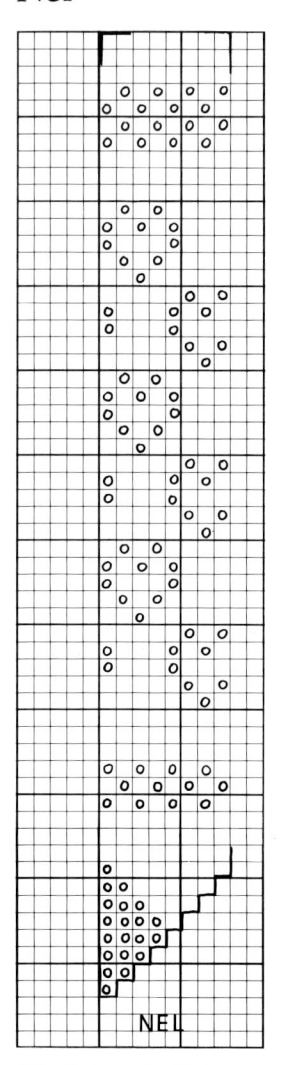

23 *Pattern for Nel (see colour plate 1)*

Wouterswoude

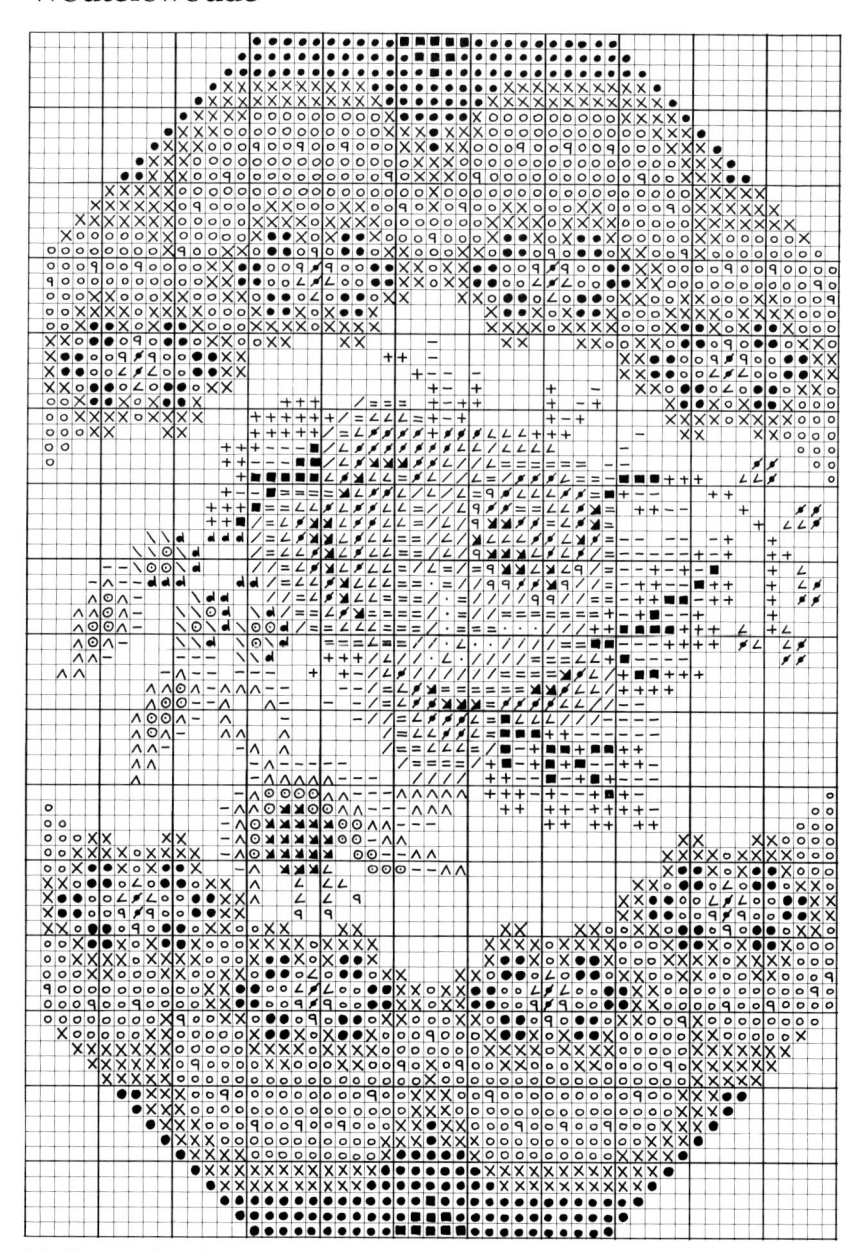

24 Pattern for Wouterswoude (see front cover)

Dog with fluffy tail

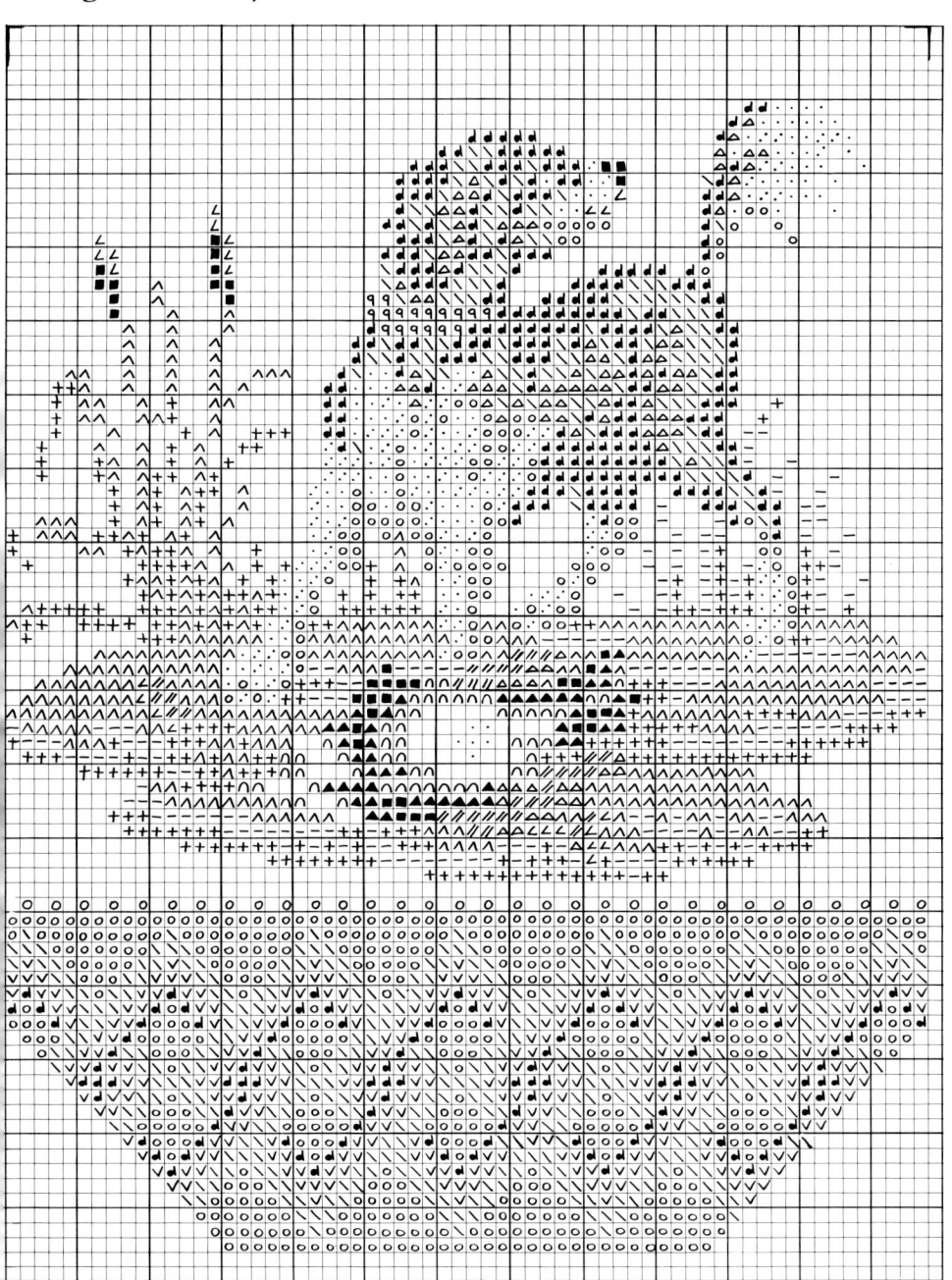

25 Pattern for Dog with fluffy tail (see colour plate 8)

< Colour plate 8 Dog with fluffy tail (see pattern diagram 25)

53

26 *Deer*